OOps!

The
Complete Book
of
Bloopers

by
Richard Smith
and Edward Decter

Illustrated by
Edie Bowers

The Rutledge Press
112 Madison Avenue
New York, New York 10016

This edition dedicated to Howie!

PRODUCED AND PACKAGED BY
DAVID M. COHN PUBLISHING, INC.
Graphics by A Good Thing, Inc., New York, New York
Editorial and Production services by Cobb-Dunlop, Inc.

Published by The Rutledge Press, 112 Madison Avenue,
New York, New York 10016
Distributed by W. H. Smith Publishers Inc., 112 Madison
Avenue, New York, New York 10016
First Printing 1981.
Printed in the United States of America
ISBN 0–8317–6617–4

Contents

Introduction

The history of the world has been a catalogue of confused actions, verbal errors and bad ideas. From the evolutionary dead-end of the duck-billed platypus to Wrong-Way Corrigan, things have not gone "just right" very often—usually its quite the opposite. Murphy's famous law, stating that whatever could possibly go wrong almost certainly will, applies not only to technology but to every other kind of human enterprise. The "A-mazing" Mets proved the law applies to baseball, and perhaps the duck-billed platypus proves it applies as well to the evolution of species. It may be that the tendency to err is a deeply rooted biological drive. One might compare history to a machine, which unwinding through the ages, dismantles itself into a heap of relics, cast-offs, and debris.

Errors, whatever their cause, make life unpredictable—and often, very amusing. It's not only a matter of decline and fall—it's also a man slipping on a banana peel and making everyone laugh. In hindsight, hare-brained "scientific" predictions, accidents involving the most unlikely coincidences, and funny slips of the tongue *are* hilarious. Some of the more amusing errors and foul-ups are included in this book.

Politics can become comedy when a congressman's savvy is measured by his ability to chew gum and walk at the same time. A triple play against the hapless Mets can transform a stadium of fans into the laughing spectators of a ridiculous slap-stick routine. Even crime is a joke when brazen muggers demand their victim write them a personal check, or when a would-be thief asks a bankteller to deliver the loot to him while he waits for it outside the bank. Some failed criminals and successful politicians blossom into wonderful—but inadvertent—comedians.

And loose lips, no matter who they belong to, blurt out the most hilarious and crazy Froudian clips. Everyone from sports announcers to statesmen can and have played this game. Richard Nixon probably felt the pit in his stomach grow after he "mis-spoke," saying, "that is a discredited *president*" instead of what he meant, a "discredited precedent." He may not have been amused by his error, but you can bet almost everyone else was! Anyone who stumbles into such a classic Freudian slip will, no doubt, feel embarrassed and chagrined for a while, but hindsight has a way of making people laugh at the clown in themselves. Perhaps even Mr. Nixon can chuckle now, looking back on that mistake.

Yesterday's disastrous errors can be a goldmine for today's amusing anecdotes. And history, instead of seeming a nightmare, becomes the banana peel humanity slips on—a joke of cosmic proportions.

So, read *OOPS* and laugh at the politicians, crooks, generals, sports announcers—those mad-cap performers in the slap-stick of history. And after you've laughed heartily at their mistakes, look at yourself for a laugh. Don't be embarrassed to see the joke in your own mistake.

1

Politics As Usual

President Gerald Ford loved sports. "Whenever I can I always watch the Detroit Tigers on radio."

Calvin Coolidge was so stingy that the chef at the White House quit; his bills were scrutinized too closely.

The most disputed election in U. S. history was in 1876 when Rutherford B. Hayes was elected by one vote in the electoral college. Samuel Tilden won the popular election by a quarter of a million votes.

Horace Greeley lost an election to Ulysses S. Grant by 750,000 votes, and died of embarrassment before Grant's inauguation.

"The children of America must not see their president smoking."
—the immortal words of President William McKinley.

President Grover Cleveland was nicknamed "The Beast Of Buffalo," not only because he was mayor of Buffalo, New York, but also because he beat his wife.

Grover Cleveland was the father of an illegitimate child and was the 22nd and 24th president of the United States.

Rutherford B. Hayes, 19th president of the United States, had a morbid fascination with his sister who was placed in an insane asylum. Hayes has been called "the most mediocre-looking man ever to run for president."

In 1920 a candidate for the U. S. presidency ran his campaign from a jail cell. Eugene V. Debs, perennial candidate and hero of the dispossessed, garnered almost a million votes, about 3½ percent of the popular vote. Running on the Socialist platform, he won not a single electoral vote.

In response to a direct summons from President Carter, David Marston, the U. S. Attorney for Pennsylvania, braved the worst snowstorm in years to get to Washington. All flights were cancelled, so Marston grabbed a train, which derailed outside Baltimore. Not one to take a presidential summons lightly, he pressed on to the capital by bus. When he arrived at the Justice Department, he was told the interview with Carter was to be his last: the President was firing him and felt it would be more considerate to do it personally rather than by letter.

In the 1962 Senatorial race, 46,000 Connecticut voters wrote-in the name of Ted Kennedy. Flattered as Kennedy was, the votes weren't counted in his column: he was running next door in Massachusetts.

A footnote to history

Members of the advance team of Americans preparing for President Nixon's visit to China were struck by a mysterious malady.

Photographs of skin eruptions on their behinds were diagnosed in Washington as poison sumac, probably from some toilet seats made of wood of the sumac plant. Of course, Mr. Nixon's "security sweeps" from then on included careful scrutiny of any toilet seat he might use.

During the summer of 1973—an especially hot one for him—President Richard Nixon received a get-well card from another head of state, wishing him a "speedy recovery from Watergate." The well-wisher: dictator-madman Idi Amin.

Warren G. Harding, 29th president of the United States, presided over one of the most corrupt administrations in U. S. history. It is rumored that his wife poisoned her husband after his first term to avoid a pending impeachment scandal.

President James Madison was diminutive in stature (5'4") but large in imagination. As our infant nation faced another military showdown with Mother England, lacking any naval forces worth mentioning, Madison suggested the U. S. rent the Portuguese fleet. But we survived the War of 1812 quite nicely without it.

Twenty-seventh U. S. president William Taft often fell asleep during public functions. Teddy Roosevelt remarked, "Taft meant well, but he meant well feebly."

Since it was built in 1867, only six prisoners have escaped from the Sante Prison in Paris. One of them was politician Leon Daudet, who walked out the front door in 1927. Knowing something about bureaucrats, Daudet had a friend call the warden with news of a pardon for Daudet. In a civil-service reflex to an authoritative voice, the official released Daudet immediately.

Alexander Hamilton and James Madison, 18th-century American statesmen, both condemned political factions. They were the founders of the leading political parties of their day.

11

Ulysses S. Grant, famed general and 18th president of the United States, hated the sight of blood. He would only eat meat if it were cooked beyond recognition. Every morning he ate a cucumber soaked in vinegar.

"Of all the dangers which our nation has yet encountered, none are equal to those which result from success of the current effort to Africanize the southern half of the country."—not-too-liberal President Andrew Johnson.

In Chicago, Governor James Thompson was introduced as "the mayor of Illinois."

During the 1976 presidential debate, Gerald Ford insisted that Poland was "not under Soviet domination."

Twenty-third American president Benjamin Harrison's children refused to attend their father's second wedding. Harrison sought to marry his niece.

President Taft was so fat that a special bathtub had to be built for him at the White House. It could hold four normal men.

"The office of vice-president is a greater honor than I ever dreamed of attaining."—President Chester A. Arthur, who succeeded to the presidency after the assassination of James Garfield. Arthur had never once been elected to any office.

Eugene V. Debs received a million votes for president while serving time in a federal prison.

During a speech in Chicago, Mayor Daley spoke about law enforcement—"The policeman isn't there to create disorder; the policeman is there to preserve disorder."

Nebraska Senator Kenneth Wherry addressed a crowd for a full hour discussing the American involvement in the war in "Indigo-China."

Governor Al Smith of New York, speaking at Sing Sing Prison: "My fellow citizens . . . (realized prisoners were not "citizens") My fellow convicts . . . (another mistake). . . . Well, anyhow, I'm glad to see so many of you here."

U. S. President Andrew Johnson avoided impeachment by one vote during his term in office.

Before the embargo on exports of grain to the Soviet Union, the Russians were selling our wheat to Italy at a tidy profit. Pressured by U. S. farmers and grain exporters, our government has allowed grain shipments to the U. S. S. R. to resume. Business is business!

Among the other scandals and corruptions during Warren G. Harding's administration, it was common knowledge that Harding had a luscious blond lover, Nan Britton, whose son was sired by him.

"I am not fit for this office and never should have been here."— President Warren G. Harding.

Convinced that no one paid attention to introductions at White House receptions, President Harry Truman put his theory to the test. Greeting each guest one evening, he mumbled, "I killed my grandmother this morning." Every guest smiled and mumbled his pleasure—with one exception. This alert gentleman, sensing Truman's joke, replied appropriately: "She had it coming."

Machiavelli, the 16th-century Italian political writer, was exiled from Florence by the ruling Medici family for his support of anti-monarchist principles. During his 16-year confinement to his home, he realized which side his bread was buttered on and wrote *The Prince*, his celebrated treatise on the ideal aristocratic rule. Just at that point the Republicans threw the Medici family out, condemning Machiavelli for his opportunism and prolonging his banishment from politics.

It was said of 26th president Theodore Roosevelt: "When he attends a wedding he wants to be the bride and when he attends a funeral he wants to be the corpse."

After serving as president, Ulysses Simpson Grant lost 16 million dollars on Wall Street.

Interviewed on television by Theodore White, former president Richard Nixon talked about a politician's techniques of projecting a favorable image on the tube. It was important, Nixon said, " . . . to get a good picture, where you're not wiping your brow." As he said this, he illustrated by wiping his upper lip.

"I am honest and sincere in my desire to do well, but the question is whether I know enough to accomplish what I desire."—The witty President Grover Cleveland.

Who said Republicans aren't liberal? Nathaniel Bordanove, a Republican candidate for mayor of Walwick, New Jersey, was elected eight days after his death.

Spiro Agnew.

President Warren G. Harding had many nervous breakdowns and visited a sanatorium for rest periods.

"They have vilified me, they have crucified me. Yes, they have even criticized me."—Mayor Richard Daley of Chicago.

In 1938, Boston Curtis was elected Republican precinct commit-teeman from Milton, Washington. Mayor Simmons of Milton, who signed as legal witness for Curtis, said he supported the candidate in order to prove that Milton voters are extremely careless. Boston Curtis was a mule.

"When a man is asked to make a speech, the first thing he has to decide is what to say."—Gerald Ford.

"If Lincoln were alive today he would be spinning in his grave." —President Gerald Ford.

"Many Americans don't like simple things. That's what they have against we conservatives."—Barry Goldwater.

"One vote is worth a hundred obscene slogans."—Richard Nixon.

"If we give up in South Vietnam, it would give up Southeast Asia, and our defense line would be driven back to the Hawaiian Is-lands."—Gerald Ford.

Senator Everett Dirksen meant well when he defended the nomi-nation of Clare Boothe Luce as ambassador to Brazil. He wanted to support his friend Luce when he said, "Why thresh old straw, or beat an old bag of bones . . . "

"Personally, I am glad that thousands of fine young Americans can spend this Saturday afternoon knocking each other down in a spirit of clean sportsmanship and keen competition."—Gerald Ford.

Speaking to a high school audience in 1974, Gerald Ford said, "You can literally move mountains, mine the oceans, master the energy of the sun, and climb the highest peak of all—world peace. It won't be easy. But the achievements of the Tinley Park Titans weren't won easily either."

Gerald Ford won an election as congressman in a small district in Michigan and became president of the United States without winning another election.

Speaking about Gerald Ford, Lyndon Johnson said, "He played too much football with his helmet off."

"London, August 9 (UPI)—Richard M. Nixon's figure was removed from the hall of world statesmen at Madame Tussaud's wax museum today and was placed in storage."

"The idea that I should become president seems to me too visionary to require a serious answer. It has never entered my head, nor is it likely to enter the head of any sane person."—President Zachary Taylor.

"The man who uncovered Alger Hiss is in California to do the same housecleaning here. Help Richard Nixon get rid of the Jew-Communists."—Gerald L. K. Smith (1950).

"I am the first eagle scout Vice-President of the United States."
—Gerald Ford.

James Madison was the only president to experience gunfire while in his office in Washington. During the War of 1812 the capital was burned. Madison boldly attempted to take command of a troop of artillery men but when he saw the desperate state of events in Washington he retreated.

"No sane person in the country likes the war in Vietnam, and neither does President Johnson."—Hubert Humphrey.

Thomas Jefferson accumulated a $10,835 tab for the wine he consumed during his eight-year presidency.

Like father, like son
When Rep. Barry Goldwater Jr. visited the Senate in 1969 he fell asleep listening to a long-winded speech. The speaker was Barry Goldwater, Sr.

A mysterious and horrifying fact
Since 1840 any U. S. president elected in a year ending in zero has either died in office or been assassinated. President Reagan was elected in 1980 and in March, 1981 an assassination attempt was made on him. If Reagan lives through his term he will be the first president elected in a year ending in zero to do so in 140 years.

"I believe President Nixon—like Abraham Lincoln—is a man uniquely suited to serve our nation in a time of crisis."—Gerald Ford, 1969.

"The police are fully able to meet and compete with the criminals."—John F. Hylan, mayor of New York City in 1922.

"I would say that I am a moderate on domestic issues, a conservative in fiscal affairs, and a dyed-in-the-wool internationalist in foreign affairs."—Gerald Ford.

President Dwight Eisenhower seriously injured his knee while attending college. He was tackling Jim Thorpe at the time.

President Dwight D. Eisenhower's favorite dessert was prune whip.

Alice Roosevelt Longworth had this to say about stingy President Calvin Coolidge: "He was weaned on a pickle."

Dwight Eisenhower, former commander of the European Theater and President of the United States, fought a very personal battle on the lawn of the White House. Squirrels would interfere with his golf putting practice and General Eisenhower had them surrounded and removed.

"I can think of nothing more boring, for the American public, than to have to sit in their living rooms for a whole half an hour looking at my face on their television sets."—President Eisenhower.

"I would have made a good pope."—Richard Nixon.

William Howard Taft was America's fattest president. During a 1910 baseball game between Washington and Philadelphia he rose at the end of the seventh inning to stretch his lumbering torso. The crowd stood to honor the standing President. Taft originated the seventh inning stretch.

The mayor of San Francisco was asked to preside at the funeral ceremonies for Julia Ward Howe. "Your attendance here, ladies and gents, in such great numbers, shows San Francisco's appreciation of good literature. This meeting is a great testimonial to the immortal author of *Uncle Tom's Cabin*—the late Julia Ward Howard!" (Harriet Beecher Stowe wrote *Uncle Tom's Cabin*.)

"Ninety-six percent of the 6,926 communists, fellow travelers, sex perverts, people with criminal records, dope addicts, drunks, and other security risks removed under the Eisenhower security program, were hired by the Truman administration."—Richard M. Nixon (1954).

"Nobody is a friend of ours. Let's face it."—Richard Nixon.

"The United States has much to offer the third world war."—Ronald Reagan in 1975.

"Whenever any mother or father talks to his child, I hope he can look at the man in the White House, and whatever he may think of his politics, he will say, 'Well, there is a man who maintains the kind of standards personally I would want my child to follow.' "
—Richard Nixon.

"We can't get the president involved in this. His people, that is one thing. We don't want to cover up, but there are ways."—Richard Nixon, 1973.

President Calvin Coolidge was often known as a tight-lip.
"Have you anything to say about Prohibition?"
"No."
"Have you anything to say about the World Court?"
"No."
"About the farm situation?"
"No."
"About the upcoming senatorial campaign?"
"No. And don't quote me."

Richard Nixon was speaking to Washington's Governor Dan Evans during Watergate in 1974. Nixon's tongue slipped and Freud would have had a field day—"Thank you, Governor Evidence ... "

"I made my mistakes, but in all my years of public life I have never profited, never profited from public service. I have earned every cent. And in all my years of public life I have never obstructed justice. And I think too, that I could say that in my years of public life, that I welcome this kind of examination because people have got to know whether or not their President is a crook. Well, I am not a crook."—Richard Nixon, 1974.

Richard Nixon once meant to say "discredited precedent" during a speech in 1974. Instead he uttered these immortal words—"That is a discredited president ... "

"You know, I always wondered about that taping equipment but I'm damn glad we have it, aren't you?"—Richard Nixon speaking to H. R. Haldeman, 1973.

Gerald Ford was so nervous on his wedding day he wore one brown and one black shoe.

"I hope that Spiro Agnew will be completely exonerated and found guilty of the charges against him."—John Connally, defending his friend Spiro Agnew.

"Each morning he would take great pains in brushing his teeth, was careful to gargle, and asked me to smell his breath to make sure he would not offend anyone on the school bus."—Hannah Nixon, mother of Richard Nixon.

Mario Procaccino was a candidate for mayor of New York City in 1969. He was trying to reach out to black voters and said, "My heart is as black as yours."

Mario Procaccino, a Democratic candidate for mayor of New York City, was at a rally endorsing his friend Frank O'Connor. "Frank O'Connor grows on you, like a cancer," Procaccino said.

"I have only two regrets: that I have not shot Henry Clay or hanged John C. Calhoun.—" President Andrew Jackson, 1837.

John Quincy Adams, the 6th president of the United States, actually finished second in the election of 1824, behind Andrew Jackson. Since there was not a majority, the House of Representatives decided the election. Adams started a trend of minority presidents.

"There is every reason to believe that our system will soon attain the highest degree of perfection of which human institutions are capable."—James Monroe, 1820.

"There is as much chance of repealing the 18th Amendment's prohibition of alcohol as there is for a hummingbird to fly to the planet Mars with the Washington Monument tied to its tail."— Senator Morris Sheppard (Texas), author of the 18th.

William Henry Harrison became president of the United States on March 4, 1841, caught cold at the inauguration and died 31 days later—serving the shortest term of any U. S. president.

Not known as a political tiger, Martin Van Buren, 8th U. S. president, had this to say about his career: "The two happiest days of my life were those of my entrance upon the office and my surrender of it."

Ninth U. S. president William Henry Harrison was a medical school dropout. As governor of the Indiana territory he specialized in cheating the Indians out of their land.

The founder of Jacksonian Democracy, Andrew Jackson, stole much of his land from the Indians and made a fortune in real estate profits.

Eleventh U. S. President James Knox Polk died of diarrhea.

Twelfth U. S. President, Zachary Taylor, was late responding to his nomination as president because he forgot to pay the postage on his letter of notification.

"I am a Whig, but not an ultra-Whig."—President Zachary Taylor.

"The nourishment is palatable."—The last words of the exciting 13th president of the United States, Millard Fillmore. (Spoken to his doctor who was feeding him.)

During the campaign of 1852, Whig opponents charged that Franklin Pierce was "the hero of many a well-fought bottle."

Fourteenth president Franklin Pierce was a compromise choice for the nomination in 1852. Stephan Douglas said, "Hereafter no private citizen is safe."

During the Mexican war, Franklin Pierce—later to become U. S. president—charged to the front lines on his horse. The horse bolted, the saddle-horn pushed into Pierce's groin, Pierce fainted, the horse broke a leg, and Pierce injured his knee (and his pride).

Thirteenth president Millard Fillmore did not have an exciting career. One of the big issues of his administration was about quantities of sea fowl excrement in Peru that could be used for fertilizer.

President Martin Van Buren was nicknamed "Martin Van Ruin" during the depression of 1840.

Thomas Jefferson often spoke about John Adams: "He is as disinterested as the being who made him."

"There are portions of the Union in which if you emancipate your slaves they will become your masters. Is there any man who would for a moment indulge the horrible idea of abolishing slavery by the massacre of the chivalrous race of men in the south?"—President James Buchanan.

"I was never popular. The popular boys were the ones who were good at games and had big, tight fists. I was never like that. Without my glasses I was blind as a bat, and to tell the truth, I was kind of a sissy. If there was any danger of getting into a fight, I always ran. I guess that's why I'm here today."—President Harry S. Truman.

President Andrew Jackson fought several duels defending the honor of his wife before entering the White House.

The first assassination attempt on any U.S. president was on Andrew Jackson by a crazed housepainter who believed himself to be the heir to the British throne.

"Jerry (Ford) is the only man I ever knew who couldn't chew gum and walk at the same time."—Lyndon Johnson.

John Quincy Adams was known to swim naked in the Potomac River. Once a woman reporter sat on his clothes in order to force Adams to give her an interview.

Those living in glass houses
James G. Blaine ran against Grover Cleveland for president in 1884. Blaine accused Cleveland of dodging his responsibilities as a soldier in the Civil War. Cleveland had hired someone to fight in his place. Despite the truth of the claim, the voters stuck with Cleveland. Blaine had done the same thing during the war.

"He was the best potato masher one could wish for."—Richard Nixon's mother, speaking of her son.

"It's the quality of the ordinary, the straight, the square, that accounts for the great stability and success of our nation. It's a quality to be proud of."—Gerald Ford.

In U. S. president Martin Van Buren's memoirs he neglected to mention even once his wife of 12 years.

2

Life in These United States

Temple and Louis Abernathy were disappointed, to say the least. They had ridden from New York City to San Francisco, 3,600 miles, causing one of their horses to die along the way; and they did it in just over two months. That was the catch: To win the prize of $10,000 they were trying for, the trip had to be made in no more than two months, and they had gone over the limit by two days. The year was 1911, when Temple was 9 and Louis 11 years old.

Another survivor was Spike O'Donnell, a Prohibition-era Chicago hood. Spike was involved in a running territorial feud with the well-armed McErlane Gang. Hearing his name called in the street one day, O'Donnell reacted with the instincts of his kind: he dropped to the sidewalk as the drugstore window behind him was shattered by Thompson sub-machine guns. Trying again, Frank McErlane killed one of Spike's gang and wounded another. But our hero wasn't present for the party. Shortly after that, McErlane wounded Tommy O'Donnell, Spike's brother, in an attack on their car, but Spike was unharmed. No quitter, McErlane sprayed 37 shots around a saloon where O'Donnell was drinking. He got two other guys, but not Spike. Finally accepting the immortality of his enemy, Frank McErlane stopped trying to bump off Spike O'Donnell.

It was visitors' day, and Cynthia Knell knew what she had to do. Moving quickly and quietly she removed the screws holding the heavy plate-glass partition, then took out the glass. Minutes later she walked calmly out of prison in Santa Ana, California, with her inmate-husband in front of seventy other prisoners and visitors

American idioms are often difficult to translate. The advertising slogan "Come Alive with Pepsi" lost something in the German translation which read "Come Alive out of the Grave with Pepsi." In certain Slavic countries the translation became "Pepsi Brings Your Ancestors Back from the Grave."

In 1974, the son of Alabama governor George Wallace told his father that he was involved in a sociological experiment for a college course. What George, Jr. *couldn't* tell Daddy was the nature of the experiment: With a black co-ed they were playing the role of an interracial engaged couple looking for their first apartment.

Over a period of many years the Collyer brothers, Langley and Homer, had become a pair of urban hermits. They collected everything and threw nothing out of their New York City home for half a century. Langley expressed his paranoia by constructing booby traps for imagined intruders, and Homer became a helpless invalid. Returning through a "corridor" between piles of newspapers and other trash one day, Langley set off one of his traps and was buried alive under a sewing machine and a weighted suitcase. Left without care and food, Homer starved to death. After their bodies were found among the debris of their lives, an investigation revealed that the Collyer brothers were wealthy eccentrics.

Baltimore was suffering a prolonged drought in 1930, and weathermen offered no hope of relief. So you could hardly blame the city's newspaper editors for thinking they had a nut on their hands when Mrs. Fanny Shields called with a promise of rain the following day. What was the basis of her prediction? The behavior of her cat Napoleon. The next day it rained; So the papers began carrying Napoleon's weather forecasts, which proved as accurate as human ones.

When Charles Schulz, originator of the *Peanuts* characters, applied for a job at Disney Studios, they turned him down. That was before his cartoons made him rich and famous, of course.

The Pledge of Allegiance to the American flag, which has become a source of controversy in recent years, was conceived as part of a Columbus Day promotion for *Youth's Companion,* a boy's magazine.

Ku Klux Klansman Jerry Paul Smith, shown a film of himself firing a pistol into a crowd of Communist Workers Party demonstrators—five of whom died—told the Greensboro, North Carolina court trying him for murder, "It's me, but I don't remember doing it." In a classic display of Southern justice, he was acquitted by a jury of his peers.

A New York City cabbie hustled Nigerian student Anthony Alugbue out of $464 for a ten-minute ride from one terminal to another at Kennedy Airport. When Alugbue arrived in California, schoolmates told him he'd been swindled and urged him to contact New York police. Detectives sent him photographs of likely suspects and he recognized his driver. Confronted with the evidence the cabbie made restitution rather than go to jail.

Before he went West to become a legend, Kit Carson was apprenticed to a saddler. Apparently his boss wasn't that impressed with his young charge: when Carson ran away the man posted a reward of one cent for his return.

To fulfill his landlady's expectation that he would leave his apartment exactly the way he found it, Joseph Pfaff ran a classified ad in a New Jersey newspaper. He was hoping he would be able to replace the live cockroaches he found when he moved in.

The police emergency squad in Marinette, Wisconsin, discovered two pet dogs near death after they had turned on their master's gas stove. As for their master, he denied it was a suicide pact.

The Department of Agriculture quickly renamed its newest cafeteria, the Alfred Packer Grill, originally dedicated to the memory of a Colorado pioneer. Somebody pointed out that Alfred's claim to fame lay in his feat of murdering and cannibalizing 5 prospectors in 1874.

George Plimpton's career as a fireworks' manufacturer lasted about as long as all the others he's tried on for fun. He created a huge Roman candle 40 inches in diameter—nicknamed "Fat Man"—which was supposed to light up the night sky over Long Island in February, 1975. But "Fat Man" decided to go the other way instead, blowing a crater ten feet deep in the earth.

The U.S. Customs Service, charged with the prevention of drug traffic into the country, confiscates airplanes used by captured drug smugglers and sells them at auction for low prices to—guess who? That's right: other smugglers. Frustrated Customs officials keep catching and selling the same planes. Smugglers who don't want to show up at a Customs auction can buy surplus DC-3s cheaply from the Pentagon. Uncle Sam profits, and the dope keeps flowing.

In 1979 the Commerce Department spent $6,000 in a study to determine whether smoking pot diminished the effectiveness of scuba divers. The government supplied the grass, too.

A Staten Island, New York speech pathologist is offering for sale a 52-minute LP record designed to "... conjure up previously learned musical experiences, and provide a welcome relief from noise pollution ..." Jerry Cammarata's record has no sound on it.

As 1984 approaches, keep this in mind: a great many Americans, shown the text of the Bill of Rights of our Constitution, label it dangerously subversive material! Typical is a high school class in Maine where more than 70 percent of the kids, unaware that the ideas were drawn from one of our nation's founding documents, offered to sign a petition to repeal them.

One of the amazing feats of professional strongman Joe Greenstein was to drive a nail into metal with a handkerchief-covered palm. Greenstein, a devoted Democrat, was so distraught at Republican Herbert Hoover's election victory in 1928, that he inadvertently performed the stunt with the nail reversed, and he drove it through his hand. Today, at 94, Brooklynite Greenstein can still demonstrate the feat—with the nail right side up.

Jerry Della Femina, head of a large ad agency, failed his college course in copywriting. Years later he had the pleasure of turning down the job application of the professor who had flunked him.

Sitting in their kitchen, the James McBrides of Denver thought they were being bombed when an object came crashing through their ceiling. The object turned out to be a 60- pound chunk of dirty ice. A police investigation uncovered its true nature: when the valves of an airliner's chemical toilet aren't working properly, the liquid leaks out and forms an icy mass until it becomes heavy enough to break off. The McBrides' "bomb" was such a mass. According to Federal Aviation Administration records, 14 of these missiles fell from the skies into inhabited areas in 1974, the worst year yet.

Jeron King Crisswell, a self-appointed prophet, must have been a little let down at the outcome of his predictions for 1977, which included the complete cessation of rain for ten months, a Black Death plague, and mass migrations to the North and South Poles for water. But don't give up on Jeron yet—he's predicting the total submersion of New York City in 1981 and the end of the world by 1999.

When a Catholic girls' school in St. Louis mistakenly received 25 copies of *The Joy of Sex* instead of *The Joy of Cooking,* which they had ordered, school authorities never said a word and the bill was promptly paid.

When four cows' heads came ashore on the beach at East Hampton, Long Island in 1978, police wondered if they had a local

When the city of Beatrice, Nebraska tested its new sewer-cleaning system in 1977, the $12,000 marvel produced some unanticipated results. Water was back-pressured so forcefully that it shot from people's toilets as high as their bathroom ceilings.

voodoo sect on their hands. The real explanation turned out to be less bizarre but still revolting. It seems *The New York Times* food editor Craig Claiborne, a local resident, had jettisoned the heads when they proved unsatisfactory for a dinner of *tete de veau vinaigrette.*

Comedian Dick Gregory and actor Marlon Brando, both devoted to minority causes, flew to Wichita, Kansas to support American Indian suspects charged with shooting F.B.I. agents in a confrontation. The crusading pair encountered only one problem: the trial was taking place in Cedar Rapids, Iowa.

Unwilling to watch his university "disgrace itself by conferring a doctor's degree upon a barbarian and a savage who can scarcely spell his own name," John Quincy Adams turned down an invitation to a Harvard ceremony in honor of President Andrew Jackson.

General Motors recently boasted that you're perfectly safe in one of the company's cars equipped with shock-absorbing bumpers . . . up to speeds of 2.8 miles an hour, that is.

Lake Lina was a natural reservoir in the hills above Juneau, Alaska. "Was"—because it disappeared in less than three days in August of 1970 in a violent earthquake.

An embarrassed couple had a hard time telling Fort Lauderdale police what they were up to before they had to call the cops. The husband explained that he and his wife had been "fooling around" when he dropped the key and the dog swallowed it—which was why the pair were handcuffed together in the nude.

The South Carolina Statehouse was shaken by a sudden impact. Investigation disclosed that eight tons of survival crackers had fallen through the floor of the fallout shelter where they had been stored for years. Commented Woody Brooks, who occupies an adjoining office, "We knew there were some crackers back there."

Ursula Beckley was under psychiatric care after trying to make a three-egg omelette. Her lawyer filed suit for $3.6 million in damages in New York State Supreme Court—all this because the Long Islander's third egg contained a baby snake.

A television interviewer asked Senator Margaret Chase Smith the following question: "What would you do if you woke up one morning and found yourself in the White House?" Senator Smith replied, "I would go straight downstairs and apologize to Mrs. Eisenhower, and then I would go right home."

In 1968 students at the University of Colorado elected to name their cafeteria the "Alfred Packer Grill." Alfred Packer was the only person in the U.S. convicted of cannibalism.

The prize was a private lunch with the governor and a game of golf with the state attorney general. The raffle was a benefit for the Minnesota Opera. The winner was Rebecca Rae Rand, a convicted prostitute and madam.

A Norfolk, Virginia lawyer had the chore of defending a person accused of sending obscene material through the U.S. Postal Service. The lawyer called the Justice Department to obtain a copy of the obscene material. It arrived two days later—via the U.S. mail.

Famous radio announcer Ed Herlihy alienated his sponsor with this reading of a commercial—"Another delicious combination for these hot days, also by Kraft, is a chilled grease sandwich and a choke."

Botanist Thomas Nuttall lacked only one qualification for his career as a pioneer scientist in the unexplored Northwest: he could never find his way home. Risking their scalps in Indian territory, members of his expeditions had to leave torches lighted to help him find their camp. When he didn't show up one night, friends went to look for him. Taking them for Indians, he fled his rescuers for three days and wandered back into camp by chance. Nuttall found out that Indians could be kind, too, when a native found him lost and exhausted. Carrying the white man on his back for three miles to the river, the brave paddled him back to camp.

In the famous painting "Washington Crossing the Delaware" there is one historical inaccuracy. The stars and stripes carried in the boat could not have existed when Washington made his historic crossing. They were made the symbol of the nation six months after the trip across the river.

Here in nutrition-conscious America we make the mistake of throwing out the greens of carrots, beets, turnips and radishes. The greens of these vegetables are often 75 to 150 percent more nutritious than the vegetables themselves.

U.S. Representative Charles S. Joelson of New Jersey noticed that the souvenirs commemorating Iwo Jima sold in Washington, D.C., were made in Japan.

In 1962, a woman wrote to Sears Roebuck complaining that the women wearing maternity lingerie in the Sears Roebuck catalogue were not wearing wedding rings. Next issue of the catalogue all the maternity models wore rings.

Are they sorry now?
The United States purchased the Alaska Territory from Russia for an average of two cents an acre. Even at this price William Seward, the man who engineered the deal, was laughed at. The Alaska purchase was originally called Seward's Folly.

Things are not easy for tourists in the United States. Unlike most foreign currency, no U.S. coin has a numerical marking.

A government clerk in Washington, D.C., made a big mistake. Instead of writing, "All foreign fruit-plants are free from duty," he wrote "All foreign fruit, plants are free from duty." The comma, substituted for a hyphen, cost the U.S. 2 million dollars.

Contractors of the Howard Hotel in Baltimore had already started to light fires in the boilers of the hotel when they noticed they forgot to install the chimney.

"Monopoly" is America's favorite board game. Parker Brothers' board members rejected the game when it was introduced to them, stating it possessed "52 fundamental errors" that would prevent its success.

Dead-eye Jesse?
The infamous Jesse James was not the greatest shot in the Old West. During a hold-up he fired six shots at a stubborn victim and missed every time. During a daring bank job he fired at a bank teller who was inches away and missed again.

The world's foremost authorities on modern art—the curators of the Museum of Modern Art in New York—placed Henri Matisse's *Le Bateau* in a prominent spot in the museum. Late in 1961 somebody mentioned casually that they had hung it upside down.

Claudius Vermilye, Jr. ran Boys Farms, Inc., a home for troubled youths. Vermilye, an Episcopal priest who extended a hand to the troubled boys in Tennessee, brought them into his fold, and then had sexual relations with them. Vermilye also videotaped his orgies and sold them to porno film distributors. The priest was arrested after a young man told the story to authorities.

Per capita, Japanese-Americans commit less crime than any other ethnic group in the United States. During World War II the U.S. Government interned a vast number of Japanese-Americans in "internment camps."

Historian Dr. Richard M. Huber had some interesting information about American success-story writer Horatio Alger Jr. Horatio was a Unitarian minister preaching in Brewster, Massachusetts in 1866. Apparently he spent a great deal of his time organizing sports and games for the young boys at the church. The elders became curious why he was not so interested in organizing anything for the girls. Horatio Alger Jr. was found to be engaging the young boys in homosexual activities and was convicted by a local committee of "the abominable and revolting crime of unnatural familiarity with boys." Alger went on to write stories in which young men succeeded through perserverance and virtue.

A train conductor approached Dwight Morrow and asked for his ticket. Morrow could not find the ticket anywhere. "Never mind, Mr. Morrow. When you find it mail it to the company. I'm sure

41

Jane Pierce, the First Lady of President Franklin Pierce, often wrote short messages to one of her dead sons.

There really was a cow that kicked over a lantern that started the Great Chicago Fire in 1871. The small step of his hoof caused more than 300 deaths and the loss of most of downtown Chicago.

you have it," the conductor said. Absent-minded Morrow replied, "I know I have it, but what I want to know is where in the world am I going?"

The forgettable Sonny Tufts was interviewed on radio and was asked about the newspaper articles which joked about Sonny being a nonentity. Sonny replied, "I don't give a goddamn what newspaper people write about me ... I'm awfully sorry about my language ... really, I'm goddamn sorry!"

Alexander Hamilton, the first U.S. Secretary of the Treasury, died in debt. He died in a duel with Aaron Burr in the same location where Hamilton's son fought and died in a duel three years before.

3

From the Police Blotter

A pair of teenage girls had been mugging women in New York City for some time, but they'd never encountered a situation like this one: Their obviously middle-class victim could produce only $4 in cash. The kids weren't going to let her off that lightly, so they insisted she write them a check. None of that "cash" trash, either; it had to be made out in their names. So it was a simple thing for the cops to pick them up when they cashed it at the bank.

A Dallas County police officer said, "We regret that the boy lost his life and feel to some degree responsible." The regrettable incident referred to was the fatal beating and stabbing of Kenneth Nile Coppinger, Jr. while he was in custody in the county jail. The young man had been mistakenly picked up on a drinking-while-driving charge, instead of his father.

Justice is usually said to be blind, but here's a case where she turned out to be deaf. In February, 1978, the judge hearing a trial in Manitoba, Canada discovered by chance that one of the jurors was totally deaf and hadn't comprehended a word of evidence. The case began to become unglued when a second juror confessed he understood only French and didn't know what was going on. His honor had to declare a mistrial when it was found that a third member of the panel understood no English and was deaf besides.

Los Angeles police still talk about the bank heist in which one of the holdup-persons was a woman who wore a see-through blouse without a bra. Questioned after their successful getaway, the teller couldn't describe the woman's face. The robbers had chosen a male teller as their victim, of course.

Police in Portland, Oregon swear it's true. To avoid attention during his 1969 holdup of a Portland bank, the robber wrote all his instructions as the teller waited. Scribbling furiously, he wrote, "This is a holdup and I've got a gun," and held the paper up for the teller to read. The message was received with a silent nod, and the cashier waited while the bandit wrote his next installment— "Put all your money in a paper bag,"—and shoved the note through the window. The patient teller wrote his reply, "I don't have a paper bag," and unobtrusively returned the note. Unnerved, the felon ran out and melted into the crowd on the street.

When police in Saginaw, Michigan pulled over a motorist on a traffic violation, they made a coup: the guy was carrying a pistol in his car. Despite his protestations that he had never seen the weapon before, the cops knew their duty and they arrested him. Imagine the officers' embarrassment when they had to let the suspect go the following day with an apology! Seems the gun had dropped out of a cop's holster into the car when they were questioning the motorist about the traffic charge.

An 81-year-old woman awoke to find a thief in her bedroom, and gamely tackled him. Imagine the intruder's surprise when he realized his victim had been his schoolteacher years earlier. After an affectionate discussion of happy school days, he took her TV set and $210 in cash.

One false move
Raymond Burles had just held up a French bank for $6,400 in cash, coolly placed the money in the little satchel he was carrying and started to walk out, when onlookers captured and arrested him. It seems Raymond had zipped his pistol in the bag with the loot.

One of the favorite stories of the Kansas City police concerns a thief who would heave a brick through a jewelry store window, grab the goodies and run. The thing was he kept doing this at the *same* jewelry store. The owner, out of desperation, installed an unbreakable plastic window. The next time the thief chucked half a cinder block at the "glass" it rebounded and hit him in the head. He was still out when the police arrived.

Jailers in Alamo, Mexico work under a heavy threat: they have to serve out the sentences of any escapees from the prison. Needless to say, Alamo is a maximum-security facility, and no one escapes.

To finance his gangster films French movie-maker Jean-Claude Dague took to robbing banks. His productions will be even more authentic when he gets out of prison.

New York City police amuse each other with the story of a stickup man who held up a bank, ran out, and jumped into a cab to make his getaway. But, unknown to him, the cab he chose was driven by a plainclothes member of the anti-crime unit. The cop had real class, however; he didn't charge the crook for the ride to the precinct house.

When a Detroit grocery store bandit jumped in his getaway car,

47

he discovered his battery was dead. A cool cat, he went back into the grocery and forced the clerk to help him get started with jumper cables.

Michael Vaccaro of Rhode Island was serving a life sentence for murder when a court decided he had to pay a $9,000 fee to a real estate firm for the sale of his nightclub. Vaccaro's unsuccessful defense: since he no longer had any rights, he claimed he was legally dead.

Over 30,000 pairs of Levi's jeans had been stolen in Santa Clara, California, and it looked like a standard garment heist. So the Associated Press staff wasn't prepared for the call they got from Doug Breuner. Seems Doug was holding the pants "hostage" to publicize his claim that the Levi Strauss Company had committed "crimes against the Jewish people." The nature of the alleged crimes was unspecified.

Convicted rapist Larry Hand brought suit against San Quentin prison officials for "cruel and unusual punishment." Two of his guards were women and he wanted them out of his sight.

Dennis Soyster's is not the usual embezzler's tale. He stole $29,000 from his employer after doctors told him he had a rare intestinal affliction that would soon cut his life short. But the medics had a different story when Soyster returned from his "final fling." Seems he was merely allergic to the gloves worn by his surgeons. Because of the unusual circumstances of his crime he was given a suspended sentence and the opportunity to pay back his employer on the installment plan.

Detroit police chuckle about the case of a tire thief whose jack gave way, leaving his hand pinned between the tire and the car's fender. His cries for help resulted in his rescue—and his arrest.

Serving a one-to-five year sentence for burglary, Ronald Terry planned to marry Beverly Sanders as soon as possible. The lovers met when Ronald forced Beverly to drive him from the scene of his crime at gunpoint.

A New York City burglar, hotly pursued on foot by cops, vaulted a fence to escape—and landed in the back yard of the local police precinct house.

Then there's the saga of J. K. Raimey, a tire dealer who was an ardent supporter of Atlanta's police. To publicize their needs, he planned to raise a large billboard atop his store, warning potential crime victims that the city's police force was "underpaid, undermanned and underequipped." Before he could get the sign up, burglars ran off with some parts of it and someone sabotaged the crane lifting the billboard. When the announcement was finally in place, Raimey bought a shotgun to defend his premises. Soon after that a crew of thieves smashed his front window, heisted $5,000 worth of tires and equipment—and didn't neglect to include his shotgun in their loot.

The eyes have it
Following a tip, Orlando, Florida's Chief of Police broke five of his officers to probationary rank after they were photographed in a topless bar. The cops claimed they were looking for "clues"; but the pictures showed them scanning the dancer's chests for the evidence.

What could have been on the mind of the skyjacker who produced a pistol and grabbed a stewardess on a flight out of New York in 1976? The ensuing dialogue went something like this, as reported later by the hostess:

> Skyjacker: "Fly this plane to Detroit."
> Stewardess: "That's where we're going: We're scheduled to fly to Detroit."
> Skyjacker: "Oh. . . . good." He put his gun back in his pocket and reclaimed his seat.

49

Detroit police tell this one of an amateur bank robber, presently a convict: the guy pushed the traditional note through the teller's window with the traditional demand that she fill a bag with cash. But he was so nervous about the bank's surveillance cameras that he added, "I'll be waiting outside; bring it out to me." Needless to say, the police got there first.

In November, 1975, a group of convicts in Mexico's Saltillo prison began digging their tunnel to freedom. Every detail of the operation was carefully planned and executed in total secrecy. The following April the ecstatic "escapees" burst through the surface —into the courtroom where most of them had been sentenced. The startled magistrates had them returned to the prison next door, with some time added to their sentences.

Though it might have provided evidence of his guilt, the Missouri Supreme Court forbade police authorities to remove a bullet from the buttocks of suspected killer Tommie Warren on the grounds that the surgery would be "unconstitutional search and seizure."

Overnight a gang of enterprising Argentinian bandits dismantled and spirited away an iron bridge crossing the Rio Parana. The next day traffic was backed up for miles around the bridge's approaches. Although the police never caught the culprits, they found the bridge: a scrap metal merchant had bought it from the bandits.

In France in 1863 Paul Hubert served 21 years of a life sentence, accused of murdering himself.

According to the New York City Police Department, most murders don't happen the way they are depicted on television or in detective novels. The offender in nine of ten cases is immediately apprehended.

Mass-murderer Juan Corona will have difficulty receiving parole. He was sentenced to 25 life sentences for killing 25 migrant farm

50

workers. This may be one of the longest prison sentences ever given.

John B. Layton, Washington, D.C. police chief, was asked, "To what do you attribute the rash of weekend robberies in our nation's capital?" The sharp crime enforcer replied, "The biggest factor is the inclination of certain individuals for acquiring funds by illegal means."

4

For Love

Discovering that her husband had betrayed her for another woman, Prague housewife Vera Czermak hurled herself from her third-floor window—and landed on her offending man, who was killed by the impact. The widow recovered from her injuries in the hospital.

In an emotional tribute to Mother's Day, the president of the Central African Republic, Jean-Bedel Bokassa, granted amnesty to all female prisoners held by his government. Not satisfied with this homage to the fairer sex, he decreed immediate execution for all male prisoners convicted of having killed women.

When Stoyan Pandov died of blood poisoning in the hospital, his wife was inconsolable. The good lady had only bitten her husband's ear playfully while they were making love.

When a divorce decree ordered Eugene Schneider of Carteret, New Jersey to divide his property equally with his wife, the furious husband did just that: with a chain-saw he cut their $80,000 house in two equal parts.

A West German court accepted a plea of temporary insanity and acquitted a husband of strangling his wife to death. Seems his wife, a crossword puzzle fanatic, kept waking him up in the middle of the night when she was stuck on a word.

Charged with murder, the Yugoslavian defendant claimed his victim had bitten him on the scalp at a wedding. He was acquitted when the judge had his head shaved, revealing the tooth marks.

When an employer in Lyon, France surprised his wife in bed with one of his employees, he fired the guy immediately. But the employee got a local labor arbitration board to rule that he was due about $800 in salary and severance pay. The furious husband appealed the case and won, because the employee was pleasuring himself on company time. It probably didn't hurt the boss's case that the Mayor of Lyon was with him when the lovers were discovered.

Good-boy singer Pat Boone appeared on the "Mike Douglas Show." Mike asked if Pat's wife Shirley toured with him on the road. Pat answered, "It seemed that my wife Shirley was always pregnant until we found out what was causing it . . ."

Felix Faure, the president of France, died in 1899 while engaged in sex with his mistress.

In January, 1978, a heavy snowfall blanketed Louisville, Kentucky. The following October the city's medical facilities were faced with an emergency situation: more births than they could handle.

When Mrs. Miller Burnette, a 69-year-old Georgian, had to be hospitalized for the implantation of a new pacemaker battery, the unexpected surgery caused more than the usual inconvenience. She had to reschedule her honeymoon with her new husband, 81.

On the theory that she could turn her husband on sexually by frightening him, a West German hausfrau hid in her spouse's bedroom closet and sprang at him when he opened the door. The terrified man crashed through his bedroom door, tripped and tumbled out a window. The hospital reported surprisingly light injuries under the circumstances.

Perhaps the attack reported by an Atlanta department store on one of its female customers was another act of passion. It seems a man had bitten her on both ankles and run off barking.

If a male angelfish finds a mate in his first season, he will live with the female angelfish he chooses for twenty-five fruitful years. If the male angelfish does not find a mate in his first year, he dies.

French composer Chausson had a brilliant career composing chamber music. He loved to ride bicycles and this was his downfall. He lost control on a steep hill, crashed into a brick wall and was killed.

A marital dispute caused a war in Africa in 1879. Chief Sirayo of the Zulus had a wife named Umhlana who left him and headed for British territory. When the Zulus went to find and kill her Britain declared war because of a border infraction.

Too much but not enough
Cassanova admitted in his memoirs that he was impotent by the age of forty.

In 1970 a German woman named Grete Bardaum bore a set of twins. One twin was black, the other white. Later it was learned that Grete had made love to a U.S. soldier and a German businessman in one day. She had ovulated twice. *Das ist ein surprise!*

Eleanor Roosevelt found sex abhorrent and for the last 29 years of her marriage to F.D.R. she refused to sleep with him. F.D.R. had an affair with Lucy Mercer, Eleanor's social secretary.

Benjamin Franklin was one of America's great statesmen and inventors but was not the nation's best family man. He did not grant permission to his daughter to marry the man she loved, he cut off his only son, and would not return to the death-bed of his wife in England when she summoned him.

5

If It's a Question of Money

During his absence from home on business in 1835, French banker Henri Bernard's wife eloped with his cashier and a lot of money. Learning of the couple's plans on his arrival home that night, Bernard raced to Le Havre to head them off before they could board a ship for America. Confronted, the lovers pleaded for their lives. But Bernard counted out ten thousand francs from their loot and gave it to the cashier in gratitude for taking the worthless woman off his hands.

In 1897 Henry B. Stuart made a loan to George Jones at a monthly interest rate of 10 percent. Stuart lost the note, but when he found it years later he sued Jones in a California court. The 1921 decision awarded him 300 billion dollars, but he could only collect $19. At the time of his death in 1938 Stuart's paper fortune amounted to over $624 trillion—more wealth than the entire world owned at the time.

You could hardly blame Joan Campbell of Adelaide, Australia for being disappointed. She'd returned a wallet containing $224 to the man who'd lost it and received a 55¢ lottery ticket as her reward. She brightened up, however, when the ticket paid $45,000.

Albert George Siegel, a Miami lawyer, conceived of a clever get-rich-quick scheme. He sent a death warning to a rich widow, instructing her where to drop a package containing $200,000 into Biscayne Bay. When he surfaced in a wet suit at the appointed time and place, he was arrested for extortion.

In 1521 the Cambridge University Press of England loaned $40 to a German printer. When the debt was cancelled in 1971, it amounted to over $117 billion dollars. The printer's descendants were allowed to pay the original amount of the loan, without the 5% a year interest.

Employees of a bank in Sherman Oaks, California were only too happy to oblige a robber who threatened them with a bomb. Fleeing the scene, the bandit was pursued by a passerby on the street. This brave soul hauled both the crook and his "package" back to the bank, where the timed tear-gas device exploded. It took hours to ventilate the fumes.

Though Gloria Sykes suffered only black eyes and other contusions in a cable car accident, she sued successfully for $50,000. The basis of her claim: mental stress caused by the accident forced her to become sexually promiscuous. At the time of the lawsuit she had already exhibited this compulsive reaction with more than a hundred men.

The Brazilian treasury decided to stop issuing the one cruzeiro bank note in 1960. At that time the treasury discovered that it cost 1.2 cruzeiros to print a one cruzeiro note.

A proofing error at the U.S. Mint caused "In Gold We Trust" to be stamped on a series of gold coins.

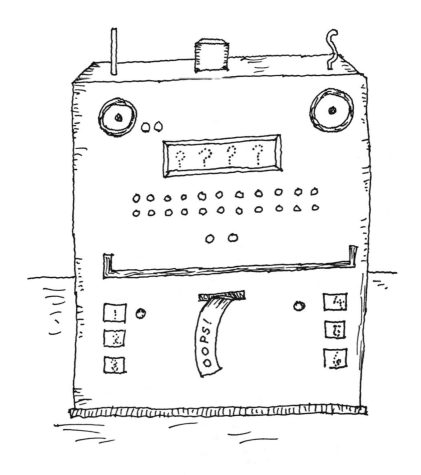

Think

Employees with accounts at IBM's company credit union in Essex Junction, Vermont, started to discover major errors in their statements. Red-faced company officials had to admit that more than a million dollars in account discrepancies were caused by computer failures.

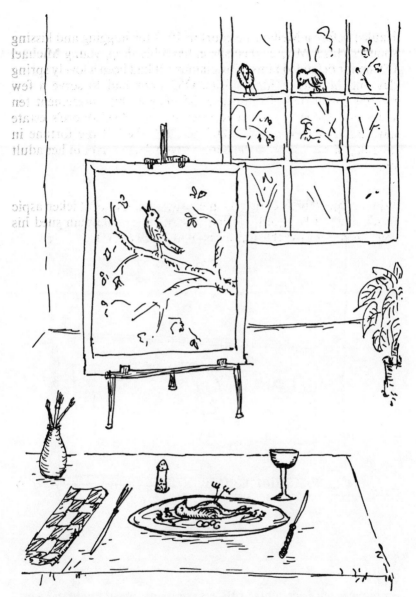

A first edition of James Audubon's *Birds of America* sold recently for $352,000. This seems like an appropriate occasion to recall that the brilliant naturalist-illustrator was so poor he often had to eat the birds he used as models for his paintings.

Hauled before a Melbourne court in 1907 for hugging and kissing spinster Hazel Moore when she entered his shop, young Michael O'Connor defended himself by claiming it had been a lovely spring day and he was in high spirits. O'Connor had to serve a few months for breach of the peace. So imagine his amazement ten years later when an attorney representing Miss Moore's estate gave him her bequest of 20,000 pounds! She left the fortune in memory of the only kiss she had received from a man in her adult life.

When young Nubar Gulbenkian charged a dinner of chicken aspic to his fabulously wealthy father, Calouste, the old man sued his son. Legal fees for the suit amounted to $145,000.

6

The Military

The famous British seaman, Lord Nelson, was seasick at the Battle of Trafalgar.

Marcus Licinius Crassus died in 53 B.C. He was an incredibly inept Roman general who led thousands of soldiers to their deaths. He was captured by the Parthians after they defeated him in battle. Later they poured molten gold down his throat.

During the Spanish-American War more American servicemen died of disease than in battle. Only 1,733 died in combat in that war, but 11,550 perished of "other causes."

In 1943 a British army officer's promotion papers were dated 1443, so he lightheartedly put in a claim for 500 years' back pay. The army replied in the same spirit: as its "oldest" officer he was billed for equipment losses dating back 500 years, which amounted to slightly more than his pay claim.

Sentenced to death in the late stages of World War II for a plot on Hitler's life, Baron von Schlavrendorff was being led from the courtroom for immediate execution. Just at that moment an Allied air raid took place. A blockbuster bomb shattered the court, killing every person in the building—except Schlavrendorff, who was unharmed and who escaped to freedom.

The Royal Navy yacht *Adventure,* rounding Cape Horn in the lead of the 1974 Round the World race, received a nine-gun salute from the British icebreaker *Endurance.* One of the shots shredded *Adventure's* headsails and the yacht's crew lost a day repairing them.

Families of married sailors in the Greek navy are due a pension if Papa dies while making love on shore leave—to Mama, of course. Unfortunately, unmarried sailors' families are excluded from the benefit.

In 1831 Edgar Allan Poe was discharged from West Point. The cadets were ordered to wear "white belts and gloves, under arms," for a parade. Poe was discharged for "gross neglect of duty" when he arrived naked except for white belts, gloves and his trusty rifle.

Ancient Iberians, abandoning their fields before Pompey's advancing legions, left the conquerors a gift: large tubs of honey. The Roman soldiers gorged themselves on the sweet prize; and when they began to succumb to the poisonous impurities the honey contained, the waiting Iberians swooped down on them from the surrounding hills.

The attack of the Spanish Armada on the English fleet in 1588 turned into one of the great military fiascos in history. A combination of savage seas and Spanish ineptness resulted in the loss of more than eighty of the Armada's 132 ships and many thousands of sailors. The tiny English fleet of 34 vessels picked apart the surviving Spanish ships, permanently altering the balance of power in the world.

In a recreational match sponsored by the Army to keep American G.I.s entertained, Carmine Milone squared off against Louis Fetters in a ring in Bristol, England. Psyched up for a quick victory, Milone charged his opponent, tripped, hit his head on a ring post and was out. Neither boxer had thrown a punch.

It was like a plot from one of his own novels: drafted into the Army in the 1950s, writer Donald Barthelme arrived in the Korean battle zone the day after the shooting was over.

The U.S. nuclear sub *Swordfish* was forced to return to drydock for repairs costing $171,000, when divers were unable to free a torpedo launcher piston. The trouble began when a 50-cent paint scraper was accidentally dropped into the launcher.

The War of 1812 between the young U.S. and its recent master, Britain, was finally concluded with a treaty of peace. But the Battle of New Orleans took place a full two weeks after it had ended, because word of the treaty hadn't reached all fronts. The battle was a resounding American victory.

During the Battle of Waterloo, British Lord Raglan suffered a severe arm wound, and the limb had to be amputated then and there. Before surgeons could dispose of the severed arm, the nobleman asked to have it back: he had forgotten to remove his wedding ring from the lost hand.

Tests of the Navy's new self-aiming "Phalanx" antimissile gun started off poorly when the weapon identified Santa Barbara Island as a target. The exercise was called off when Phalanx prepared to sink the destroyer *U.S.S. Hollister.*

General Stirling, a great American leader during the Revolutionary War, was a very serious alcoholic. It is conjectured that his aide, James Monroe, learned how to drink from Stirling. Monroe went on to become the 5th president of the United States.

General Horatio Gates was a genearal during the American Revolutionary War. He was such a bad commander that he ordered his troops to stay in their tents rather than do battle with the British. Luckily, his assistant, Benedict Arnold, disregarded orders and won the Battle of Bemis Heights and the Battle of Saratoga. Unhappily for the Americans, Benedict Arnold switched sides. Without his aid, Gates blundered in the Battle of Camden and was booted out of the American Army.

Often a player on your team is more of a help to the opponent. Such was the case of American General William H. Winder during the War of 1812. After losing the battle of Stony Creek (the Americans had four-to-one troop superiority), he was captured by the British. Realizing that they had captured their biggest asset, the British released Winder, hoping he would bring more disaster to the Americans. The British strategy proved effective. Winder was put in charge of defending the nation's capital. The capital was raided and burned to the ground.

General Ambrose Burnside was a thorn in the side of the Union Army during the Civil War. General Burnside caused the Union to lose three major battles under his inept leadership. He ordered an entire troop to travel over a small bridge where hundreds of the Confederate gunners picked them off. The bridge crossed a river so shallow that any man could wade across without wetting his belt. This "battle," the Battle of Antietam, is now synonomous with the word "mistake." At Fredricksburg, Burnside sacrificed 1,200 men in a frontal attack. At Petersburg, Burnside ordered his men into a large pit which the Confederate troops surrounded, shooting the Union soldiers like fish in a barrel. "Only Burnside could have managed such a coup, wringing one last spectacular defeat from the jaws of victory."—Abe Lincoln.

During World War I, General Sir Ian Hamilton of Britain made the mistake of vacationing on a Greek island while he should have been supervising the attack on Constantinople. His laziness and ineptitude caused 250,000 French and British soldiers to die.

General Irvin McDowell was a general of the Union Army during the Civil War. He commanded both battles of Bull Run which were huge defeats for the North. He was taken out of active duty after his failures.

George Washington speaking in 1776 at the inception of the Revolutionary War: "The war depends, in all human probability, on the exertion of a few weeks."

It seems the French have a history of poor military leadership. General Maurice Gamelin was the French Army Commander in Chief in the beginning of World War II. Gamelin watched as the Nazis rolled through Belgium. He decided to stay behind the antiquated Maginot Line, a stationary line of gun implacements left over from World War I. The guns at the Maginot Line could only shoot in one direction, and the lightning strike of the German Blitzkrieg nullified its effectiveness. France was taken in a matter of weeks, Gamelin was relieved of his command.

For all the press that General Santa Anna received, he was a lousy commander. He lost two wars for Mexico—the Mexican-American War and the Texas War. He once set up camp with his roving band of fighters one mile from the entire Texas army. He looked better in the movies.

General Stonewall Jackson of the Confederate Army went on a scouting mission at night to find a way to attack the Union army. On his return, he was killed by a Confederate sentry who did not recognize his general.

Colonel David Marcus of the Israeli Army died in 1948 as he was urinating outside his tent. He was killed by his own soldiers because they thought he was an Arab. Marcus had a bedsheet wrapped around himself as he urinated.

In 1628 the Swedish Navy constructed the largest battleship of the age called the *Vasa*. It had 64 guns on its two decks. Moments after it was launched, the top-heavy boat sank, killing 50 people.

In 1925 a Greek soldier's dog ran across the Greek border into Bulgaria. A Bulgarian border guard shot the Greek soldier. The Greeks invaded Bulgaria. The League of Nations had to arrange a truce between the two countries.

Gun's don't kill people; people kill people
When the United States Army left arms behind at bases in Thailand the violent crime rate of that country increased several thousand times.

General Aleksander Samsonov could do nothing right. He was a lazy bureaucrat who was promoted to general. He could not find the enemy during his command of the Russian Second Army in World War I. The Germans slaughtered his troops at Tannenberg. Samsonov was ashamed and tried to ride into the front line of attack, hoping he would be killed in battle. He failed in this attempt also. Finally he did something well—he managed to commit suicide in 1914.

During World War I, the French suffered a huge defeat in the Battle of Verdun. General Robert Nivelle assumed command of the ragged French Army. His first decision was to mount another huge offensive. He continued to order waves of soldiers to the front. The French finally mutinied; Nivelle was dismissed after causing thousands of unnecessary deaths.

Aleksei Kuropatkin was a Russian general in the Russo-Japanese War in 1904. He lost every battle he commanded.

70

At the battle of Fort Sumter, the first battle of the Civil War, General P.G.T Beauregard forced the surrender of Union garrison leader Major Robert Anderson. Anderson had been the instructor of Beauregard at West Point, and out of courtesy the southern general let Anderson escape. The single casualty of the battle was a luckless soldier who fired a cannon in tribute to the Union.

Arlington National Cemetery, near Washington, D.C., has started work on the fourth tomb of the unknown soldier to honor the men killed in action in Vietnam. Only one problem—there are no unknown soldiers. All those Americans whose bodies were found have been identified.

Inept commander Colonel John Finnis was killed by his own troops in 1857 after he had lectured them about insubordination. He was a commander of the British Army in India at the time.

Greek soldier Pheidippides ran the first Olympic "marathon." He was the messenger sent from the battle of Marathon to Athens—a distance of 26 miles 385 yds., the length of the modern Olympic event—with the news of the victory. As he burst into Athens with the jubilant news of the Greek victory over the Persians, he cried out, "Rejoice we conquer," Pheidippides then immediately died.

In 1943 the Allied armies planned the attack of Italy after the victory in Sicily. The plan called for a landing at Anzio beach outside of Rome. For three days and nights huge American battle-ships pounded the beach at Anzio with shells. When the landing took place the U.S. and British soldiers discovered that there had been no Germans at Anzio beach at all. The three day bombardment resulted in the death of several civilians and farm animals. The delay at Anzio impeded the Allied army's march to Rome. The blunder gave the German army time to regroup around the Italian city.

7

Star Performers

Hector Berlioz was conducting a full program of music at the *Theatre Italien,* whose rules permitted musicians to stop work at midnight. As the bewitching hour approached, a considerable part of the program remained to be performed. Berlioz turned to the orchestra just after midnight to conduct his own *Symphonie Fantastique* and found twelve musicians left. Explaining to the audience that his work couldn't be performed by so small a group, the embarrassed composer had to call the concert off.

Bronco Billy Anderson, star of the first classic American western movie, *The Great Train Robbery,* had to be helped into the saddle.

A French vaudevillian named Le Petomane drew enormous crowds to his performances at the celebrated Moulin Rouge for over twenty years. He was the world's most talented farter; he imitated famous opera singers, played the ocarina, blew out a candle a foot away and roused his audiences to a patriotic frenzy by playing the national anthem on his derriere.

During a regular cockfight in Manila, the Philippines, one of the trained birds attacked and killed the referee.

Passenger Jack Sharin was wedged in the partition window between the front and back seats of the Chicago cab he was riding. How did he get stuck there, you want to know? Seems he made a desperate dive for the wheel when his driver fell out of the cab on a turn.

Composer Franz Schubert produced so much music so rapidly that he sometimes couldn't recognize his own work when it was shown to him.

Fire totally destroyed a California movie theater despite the best efforts of firemen. The picture on the screen: *The Towering Inferno.*

What are the odds on this one? The scene was Paris, at the opening of the opera *Charles VI* in 1849. As the aria "O God, Kill Him!" began, one of the performers dropped dead on stage. At the same point the following night a member of the audience died of a stroke. When the orchestra conductor succumbed to a heart attack at the start of the aria on the third night, Emperor Napoleon III nervously closed the show.

Moliere, the great 17th-century French satirist, died while playing the role of the hypochondriac in his play *The Imaginary Invalid.*

At age 21, singing star Elton John botched a suicide attempt after the breakup of his relationship with a statuesque blonde. The way he describes it today it was a "Woody Allen-type suicide." Seems he turned on the gas jets but left the windows open.

Montana State University physics professor Larry Kirkpatrick keeps his students' attention riveted by lecturing to them from a bed of nails. He has learned how to lie on 3,739 one-inch nails without being punctured. He occasionally invites a bored student to sit on his chest. Kirkpatrick offers the scientific explanation that his weight is distributed among so many nails that the pressure exerted by any one isn't sufficient to break his skin.

In 1938 Douglas Corrigan earned immortality by taking off in his plane from New York bound for Los Angeles, and landing in Dublin, Ireland the next day. He also earned the lifetime nickname of "Wrong-Way" for his stupendous error, which he blamed on a mistaken compass setting.

To the shock and dismay of his family, a wealthy Scotsman named Malcolm announced at a Christmas party in 1832 that he was planning to marry his housekeeper. The shock was because everyone knew Malcolm despised his shrewish housekeeper, though she'd been in his service 40 years. The dismay was due to the disappointed hopes of his prospective heirs. What none suspected was Malcolm's grim sense of humor: he knew he was close to death and would never marry the woman, but he wanted to raise her hopes and then dash them with his death. The housekeeper, it seems, was shrewd as well as shrewish. She claimed and won Malcolm's fortune on the basis of an ancient Scottish law that gave marital status to a woman once a man had publicly acknowledged he would marry her.

Who Is This Character?

There *is* some truth to the old adage that there is many a slip twixt the cup and lip. In 1959, novice anchorman Grant J. Austin (a.k.a. James A. Grenzebach) of Lima, Ohio, announced to his WIMA/TV audience: "Ladies and gentlemen stay tuned for Matt Basterson, next on NBC." Needless to say, the studio howled!

Spotting a suspicious criminal type racing through Greenwich Village streets, an alert New York City cop slowed the suspect down with a blow from his nightstick. The cop was immediately surrounded by a screaming, gesticulating mob. His victim was actor James Coburn, doing a scene for a movie.

No one would guess from actor Bela Lugosi's grisly horror movie roles that he became sick and faint at the sight of his own blood.

Anthropologist Margaret Mead was one of the most active lecturers in the world, so she could be forgiven for occasionally mistaking the nature of her audience—like the time she mistook a group of theologians for professional anthropologists and lectured to them about sexual deviations among the Tchambuli of New Guinea. Not one of her ecclesiastical listeners was inclined to protest.

At the height of the anti-war campus demonstrations in 1973, students at the State University of New York at Buffalo were warned by police against throwing an effigy of President Nixon over the Falls into the Niagara River. The legal threat was an antipollution statute.

The memorial statue erected in Vienna to the memory of composer Franz Schubert cost more than the luckless genius earned from his work during his lifetime.

Actors "between engagements" are entitled to receive unemployment compensation, no matter how high their salaries when working. Suave character actor Adolphe Menjou wasn't embarrassed to pick up his unemployment checks in a chauffeured Rolls Royce.

Sam Goldwyn, the movie mogul, wasn't a reader, but he did have one favorite book. He owned the movie rights to the book but saw no point in producing a fairy tale, so he sold the rights to MGM's Louis Mayer. The book: *The Wizard of Oz.* The rest is movie history.

After asking his father-in-law the identity of the delicious meat they were eating, Amaro Maturano, an Argentinian, went on a rampage. He set fire to a truck and farmhouse, beat three cows and nine mules to death and broke the necks of forty chickens. He must have been a dog-lover, because that's what he'd been eating.

After hearing the first several songs for the new musical, *My Fair Lady,* Mary Martin turned down an offer to play the lead role of

77

Eliza Doolittle. She shared with her husband her misgivings that composers Alan Jay Lerner and Frederick Loewe had lost their talent.

Scheduled to play a concert in the Baltic port of Riga, the traveling orchestra arrived in the middle of a furious storm. The conductor got the concert manager to agree that the engagement would be canceled if no one showed up at the hall. This would permit the musicians to catch an early boat to their next date in Helsinki, Finland. But someone did show up; a single elderly gentleman sat smiling, waiting for the performance. The manager insisted that the musicians fulfill their contract, so they played the entire program for the lone listener. At the end the old man didn't stir to leave; when approached he was found to be dead! Even stranger was the aftermath: the boat the musicians missed to play for a dead man had sunk with no survivors.

More recent successes have almost erased the memory of our Mariner I space probe—but not quite. Designed to explore Venus, its computer program included complete instructions for the robot craft: booster acceleration, solar cell display, course corrections—everything. Four minutes after liftoff from Cape Canaveral on July 28, 1962, Mariner I disappeared into the Atlantic. The omission of a minus sign from its computer program was responsible for the costly failure.

In June of 1978 Bob Specas was preparing to test the domino theory: in front of TV cameras he would try to topple 100,000 dominoes just by pushing the first one in line. One by one the little black tiles were laboriously set up in a row in a studio in New York's Manhattan Center. About 97,000 of them were set when a reporter dropped his press badge and triggered off the desired chain reaction. The feat was never recorded on film.

In 1962 Martin Reilly of Pittsfield, Massachusetts burned his own eighteen-room house to the ground to avoid paying property taxes. The town still pressed its tax claim against Reilly.

Rodney Dangerfield gets no respect. He asked his son what he would most like for his birthday. His son said, "to be an orphan."

"My grandson was so ugly when he was born, the doctor slapped his mother."—Henny Youngman.

One New Year's Eve the Tonight Show's producers placed a remote camera unit on Times Square in New York City to record the festivities. Just before midnight Johnny Carson announced to five million viewers, "We now will switch you to 42nd Street and Broadway for a Times Square pickup."

Medical mistake
"A doctor gave a man six months to live . . . he couldn't pay his bills . . . so the doctor gave him another six months."—Henny Youngman.

In 1962, the quotable German President Lubke greeted the president of India at the airport with this question, which he had deftly translated into English—"Who are you?" Lubke had meant to say "How are you?" but his Indian guest was not rattled, and replied, "I am the president of India."

One would hope that the United States ambassador to Great Britain could speak the language. When Queen Elizabeth asked a nervous American ambassador, Walter Annenberg, about his London accommodations, he replied that he was having "some discomfiture as a result of a need for elements of refurbishing."

Standing before a marching band moments before a royal reception was about to begin, Germany's president, Heinrich Lubke, turned to Queen Elizabeth II and attempted to translate "Gleich geht es los" ("It will soon begin") into the Queen's English. Proudly, he told the queen, "Equal goes it loose."

Virginia Graham hosted an NBC talk show in the 1950s. She and

Angie Dickinson were discussing motherhood when Virginia asked Angie about her child, "How old was she when she was born?"

"This is Art Linkletter saying good night . . . and a special thanks to you, Edith Head, and your girls for bringing your dresses down on our program."

Kirk Douglas's agent forced his client to turn down the lead role in *Cat Ballou* (1965). Lee Marvin played the role and won the Oscar.

A frightening thought—Raymond Burr was once a professional nightclub singer.

One of the most lucrative game show series on television lasted just 15 days on ABC in 1963. It was called *"One Hundred Grand."*

Ed Sullivan liked to help out young talent. He often would introduce stars who graced his audiences. One night Ed had the lights turned up and announced, "Sitting out in our audience is talented Dolores Gray, currently starving on Broadway."

A New York woman artist who describes herself as "a multimedia performance artist," started an unusual project in 1979. She decided to shake hands with the 8500 sanitation men of New York. She photographed and videotaped the glamorous event.

Famous fashion designer Oleg Cassini presented a fashion show on Johnny Carson's "Tonight Show." As a beautiful model passed down a runway, Oleg described her outfit: "This is a lovely hostess dinner dress with a very low neckline for easy entertaining."

Ed Sullivan was not known for his ethnicity, but he introduced one champion skier on his show as "the world sholom champion."

One evening Ed Sullivan closed his show with a public service announcement—"And now a word about tuberculosis . . . Good night everybody . . . and help stamp out T.V.!"

Conservative Senator Barry Goldwater appeared on the "Joey Bishop Show" and Joey asked the Senator if he would like to become a regular on the show. Barry replied, "No, thank you, I'd much rather watch you in bed with my wife."

Mark Twain missed by a day. "I came in with Halley's Comet in 1835. It's coming again next year, and I expect to go out with it. It will be the greatest disappointment of my life if I don't go out with Halley's Comet. The Almighty has said, no doubt: 'Now here are these two unaccountable freaks; they came in together, they must go out together.' " Halley's Comet reached it's peak April 20th, 1909. Twain died on April 21st.

Dick Cavett used to host a show called "This Morning" on ABC. Dick's guest one morning was Christine Jorgensen, the famous transsexual. She explained to Dick that "sex is not determined by genitals alone." Unwittingly the host replied, "I don't think I quite grasp that . . ."

David Hartman of the Good Morning America television show made the sponsors' hearts jump when he segued into a commercial saying, "We'll be right back after this word from General Fools."

One sign of chess master Wilhelm Steinmetz's advancing insanity was his public challenge to play a match against God. Not that he disliked the Lord, mind you; in fact they had frequent conversations. But Steinmetz was definitely showing off when he offered the Almighty a one-pawn handicap.

CBS anchorman Walter Cronkite made this slip,—"Prayers were offered throughout the world as Pope Paul planned for prostate surgery at the Pentagon . . . that should be the Vatican." Cronkite (the sound of) translates as "sickness" in German.

81

"Gold's Law—If the shoe fits, it's ugly."—Arthur Block.

"I went to a fight the other night and a hockey game broke out."
—Rodney Dangerfield.

A nervous Kaye Stevens made her television singing debut on the
"Jack Paar Show." After finishing her number, Paar asked her if
this actually was the first time she had performed on television.
She answered, "I was a virgin until I appeared on your program,
Mr. Paar!"

Walter Cronkite read this blurb straight off the teleprompter—
"Rolls-Royce announced today that it is recalling all Rolls-Royce
cars made after 1966 because of faulty nuts behind the steering
wheels."

Ninety-five out of one hundred Americans have not seen a live
professional stage production. Who buys all those $45.00 tickets?

It ain't the meat it's the motion
The first time Richard Burton kissed beautiful Elizabeth Taylor
was during the filming of the costume-epic *Cleopatra*. At the
momentous moment, when the two stars' lips met, Elizabeth Taylor burped. Cut!!

Angry youth actor James Dean really dug into his roles. In the
beginning of *Rebel Without a Cause* Dean punches a desk with
his fist. He broke two fingers.

Life imitates Art?
Pancho Villa, the guerilla warrior, signed a contract with Mutual
Films of New York on January 3, 1914, giving Mutual exclusive
screen rights to film Villa's guerilla war. The Mexican received
$25,000 and a share of the gross. In the contract, Villa agreed to
attack during daylight for good exposure, and at one point he

82

waited for a film crew before he attacked Ojinaga. He made all the arrangements without an agent.

Marlon Brando turned down the lead role of Frankie in *Man with the Golden Arm.* Frank Sinatra played the part.

Bette Davis thought Errol Flynn was going to star in *Gone with the Wind,* so she turned down the role of Scarlet O'Hara. Vivien Leigh played the role and won an Oscar.

It is rumored that the original cast of *Casablanca* was supposed to include Ronald Reagan and Ann Sheridan. In retrospect this would have been the greatest mistake in the history of mankind.

Television actor James Arness was ordered to jump off the landing barge first at the Battle of Anzio beach in World War II. He wasn't chosen to be the first American in that battle for his looks; he was the tallest man on board and his commander wanted to see if the water was too deep.

Graham Kerr, the host of the "Galloping Gourmet" cooking show, was preparing a squid dish on the air when his tongue galloped away from him: "A squid, as you know of course, has ten testicles . . ."

The comedy team of Jerry Lewis and Dean Martin made many memorable movies. They also had many memorable out-takes during the shooting of those movies. While shooting a commercial for their Paramount film, *The Caddy,* Dean Martin read off the cue cards, "*The Caddy* is one of the most righteous pictures you will ever see." Jerry Lewis immediately cut his partner off. "Righteous? Where the fuck do you see 'righteous?' That's *riotous,* you greaseball!"

During his radio years Bob Hope talked about summer fashion: "Women are wearing bathing suits so short this year that they'll have to get two haircuts."

83

Famed American dancer, Isadora Duncan, wore a long scarf during a ride in a convertible car. The scarf caught in the spokes of the wheels and she broke her neck and died in 1927.

Johnny Carson on the "Tonight Show" introduced comedienne Shari Lewis: "And now a girl who is one of the bust pepiteers, in the business!"

During the "daytime News" on NBC a newsman read, "The rumor that President Nixon would veto the bill comes from high White Horse souses."

Jimmy Dean introduced the voluptuous singer, Abbe Lane, on the "Tonight Show": "Abbe Lane is a very beautiful girl with two great things going for her."

Of all the luck
The actual "Birdman of Alcatraz," Robert Stroud, was refused permission to view the Burt Lancaster movie based on Stroud's life.

Harry Von Zell, announcing the winner of the presidential election for the first time on radio: "Ladies and Gentlemen, the President of the United States—Hoobert Heever."

Someone introduced comedian Ed Wynn to the hostess of a party: "This is Ed Wynn, who's not such a fool as he looks." "That's right," snapped Wynn. "That's the great difference between me and my friend."

Censors once deleted the word "diarrhea" from the *"Tonight Show"* starring Johnny Carson.

Censors dictated that Barbara Eden of *"I Dream of Jeannie"* tape her navel so that it would not show in her revealing costume.

Remember?

In 1956, T.V. censors would not permit Elvis Presley's hips to be shown on the "Ed Sullivan Show." They claimed Elvis' gyrating hips would be *too sexy.*

The one and only collaboration of Jerome Kern and Victor Herbert was a Broadway show called *Miss* in 1917. Despite the work of two brilliant musicians, the show flopped badly.

In 1973 anti-war drama *Sticks and Bones* was censored by CBS affiliates. The affiliates claimed the Tony-award winning drama might offend relatives of POWs.

June Brown hosted a television series on ABC called *"Penthouse Sonata."* The series ran for only eight days.

When comedienne Carol Burnett appeared on the "Merv Griffin Show" in 1969, censors cut her appeal to the public to write letters to Mrs. Martin Luther King, Jr.

Myrna Loy turned down the lead of *It Happened One Night,* Frank Capra's American film masterpiece. Claudette Colbert played Ellie Andrews and won an Academy Award. Myrna Loy thought the film would fail because it took place on a bus. The movie was one of the greatest successes in movie history. A bad career choice for Myrna.

Burt Lancaster turned down the lead in a movie called *Ben-Hur.* Charlton Heston played Judah Ben-Hur and won an Oscar.

Censors deleted the phrase "stretch marks" from NBC's comedy series "Fay" starring Lee Grant.

Some say that George Raft had a hand in making Humphrey Bogart a star. Raft turned down the leads in *High Sierra, The Maltese Falcon,* and *Casablanca.* Most Americans remember Bogart and not Raft.

Eva Marie Saint turned down the lead in *Three Faces of Eve.* Joanne Woodward won an Academy Award for the role of Eve.

ABC censors deleted the phrase "naughty-bits" from a sketch during an episode of "Monty Python's Flying Circus."

Durwood Kirby appeared on "Candid Camera," hosted by Allen Funt. Kirby segued from the commercial like this, "And now back to Alice Funt."

Censors deleted a bikini contest on a 1969 edition of *"Wide World of Sports."* They claimed the film to be of "poor quality."

A major Hollywood blunder
Lauren Bacall, one of the most alluring, talented and sassiest stars of the silver screen, was never nominated for an Academy Award.

Sex-symbol Raquel Welch appeared on Johnny Carson's "Tonight Show," walking on stage with a white kitten. She sat in the guest seat next to Johnny and placed the cat across her lap. Johnny noticed the cat and Raquel asked him, "Do you want to pet my pussy?" Johnny leered and said, "I will if you move the damn cat!"

Thomas Mann, the author of *Death in Venice,* found himself dancing with a famous photo model. She wanted to impress the world famous author. She looked up into his eyes and said, "I just love culture, don't you?"

8

That's Life

From 1906–1915 Mary Mallon, a.k.a. Typhoid Mary, worked as a cook in New York City and spread typhoid through the food she served.

Testifying before a congressional committee investigating health effects of the 1951–1963 nuclear above-ground tests conducted 80 miles from her Nevada ranch, Mrs. Martha Laird said that her family had never been warned about radiation. Both her husband and son contracted leukemia, and her son died. Repeated attempts to get a satisfactory reply from government agencies bore no results except the sinister suggestion that her complaints were inspired by Communists.

When a Florida couple bought three tons of sewage sludge to fertilize their lawn, they couldn't have predicted the outcome. Instead of a carpet of grass they had thousands of tomato plants!

Trying to figure it out, they came to this conclusion: Because tomato seeds aren't digested in the human body, they passed intact through people's intestines on their way to the couple's lawn.

Hotrods, U.S.A.

Because the U.S. Government has discovered no safe way to dispose of the radioactive spent fuel rods from nuclear reactors, over 3,000 tons of the things are being stored, "temporarily," underwater in concrete tanks. If present plans for expanding nuclear plants are carried out, about 150,000 tons of these "hotrods" will be on our hands by the end of the century.

Auto recalls are bad enough, but how about this one? We sure hope you weren't one of the 552 heart patients who had just undergone chest surgery for a pacemaker implantation when the manufacturer discovered they "might be" defective. Along with this bold admission, the American Pacemaker Corporation offered its recommendation that, "consistent with good patient management," their faulty product should be removed from the patients and replaced. We know who suffered the pain, but we find ourselves wondering who paid the bill for the necessary operations.

The famous conductor, Jean Baptiste Lully, would pound out the rhythm to his orchestra by stamping a long-pointed cane on the floor. One ill-fated morning he missed the floor, speared his foot, contracted blood poisoning, and died.

What a trip

A lively South African had a body that just wouldn't quit. Attempting to commit suicide, he was still alive after swallowing a jar of sleeping pills, slashing his wrists, shooting himself in the head and hanging himself. Exasperated, he finally found the fatal formula: a deep draught of hydrochloric acid.

Famed Russian composer Alexander Scriaban let a pustule on his lip become infected, and it turned into a large carbuncle. From his little injury he contracted blood poisoning and died.

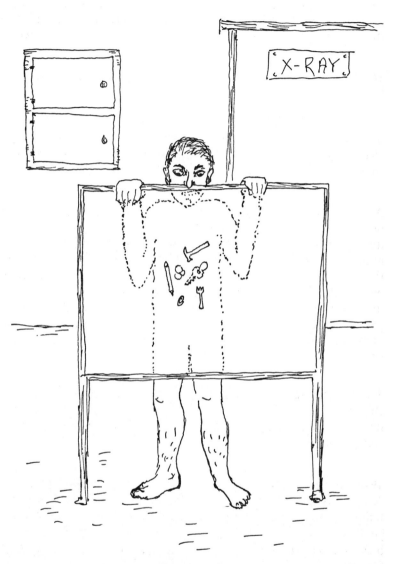

The American Medical Association's journal reported an unusual case to its readers in 1960. It seems a patient admitted for complaining of a swollen ankle also had some tummy problems. X-rays revealed he had swallowed 258 separate objects, including nail files, coins and keys.

If a man would eat only celery or lettuce as his diet he would die of starvation. It takes more energy to eat these vegetables than they return to the body.

Before he was thirty George Washington suffered from malaria, smallpox, pleurisy and dysentery.

An Australian marathon was sponsored by the Anti-Careless Accident Campaign of Southwestern Australia. The marathon was designed for a crew of young doctors and nurses to push a hospital bed from Perth to Hobart. A nurse fell in front of the moving bed and broke her neck.

In the early years of X-ray technology, Elizabeth Fleischman Ascheim worked as an X-ray technician and often demonstrated to her patients how harmless the rays were. In 1905 she died of severe skin cancer.

Two-time Nobel prize-winner Marie Curie died of radiation poisoning in 1934.

The famous physician Semmelweis, who fought against operating room contamination by unclean doctors, died of an infection caused by cutting his hand with dirty dissection instruments.

In 1890 a man in Sweden sold his own body (while still alive) for dissection after his death. He then inherited some money and decided he wanted to recover possession of his corpse. The Government refused. The man also had to pay damages for the merchandise he sold—he had had two teeth pulled.

Dr. Charles Gullett, writing in the *Journal of the American Medical Association,* warned that the silicone bags surgically implanted to enlarge women's breasts could swell in size during an air flight. The bags, adjusted to sea-level pressures, could even explode in the event of cabin depressurization, he said.

A housewife in King's Lynn, England wrote to the producers of the TV comedy show "The Goodies" to thank them for making her husband's last minutes so happy. It seems that hubby had died of a heart attack in a fit of laughter while watching the show.

Another Argentinian tale deals with eating, too, but it ends more happily. When a passenger train struck a cow in Cordoba and derailed, several years ago, the imaginative people dug a barbecue pit and roasted the animal while waiting for the repair crew to arrive.

Out where men are men—in Wind Lake, Wisconsin—they still talk about Teryl Barth. Showing off for the boys at his favorite saloon, Barth had the bartender set up a round of five different liquors: 80-proof brandy, 90-proof Jack Daniels, 100-proof Southern Comfort, 100-proof Yukon Jack and 150-proof Myers rum. He tossed down the shots one on top of the other and ordered another round. By the third round he had the attention of all fifty customers. By the fifth round the crowd was betting on the outcome. After four hours of non-stop drinking, good ol' Terry was slowing down. He downed his 46th shot and collapsed. Good ol' Terry was 19 when he died a short time later.

Along with all the other problems of motherhood, fetuses have been known to get the hiccups.

Hot stuff
At the time of his death Congressman Leo Ryan had been investigating radioactive waste disposal in the U.S. He had discovered that almost 75 million gallons of high-radiation waste were stored "temporarily" in steel drums since 1944. Between 1958 and 1975 about half a million gallons of the material had already leaked into our water supplies.

In August, 1980, two chiropractors drove to a healing meditation service in Springfield, Massachusetts, because one of them had recently suffered a stroke. The service was so relaxing that the one who was driving home fell asleep at the wheel and plowed into a tree, completely demolishing the car. Strangely enough, the two occupants were unhurt.

"The coupling of a contaminated system with a portable water system is considered poor practice in general." Workers at a nuclear power plant might have stated the conclusion more strongly than the official investigators. It was discovered that one of their drinking fountains was hooked up to a 3,000 gallon radioactive waste tank instead of a fresh water supply.

Desperate sailors often attempt to drink sea water. Sea water is so salty the body must produce three times as much urine to drain the salt out of its system. Drinking sea water dehydrates the body faster than no water at all.

Peter Sellers' death in 1980 recalls his earlier heart attack, when doctors at Los Angeles' Cedars of Lebanon Hospital declared him clinically dead six times but revived him each time with their special procedures and equipment.

9

Firsts

Bard bobble
In Shakespeare's *Julius Caesar,* Brutus says, "Tis strucken eight," when asked what time it is. There were no striking clocks in Caesar's time, only in Shakespeare's time.

Try to say this: "The sixth sick sheik's sixth sheep's sick."

The original Wright Brothers' plane is on exhibit in London's Kensington Museum, not in the U.S. The Wrights sent it overseas in anger, when our own Smithsonian Institution failed to recognize theirs as the first successful flight. The Smithsonian awarded the honor to Samuel P. Langley instead. Though Langley took to the air the same year as the Wrights, it's generally believed they flew first.

Claude Rains' film *The Invisible Man* was made with some of the cleverest special effects possible in its time, and it played to considerable critical acclaim. But observant filmgoers couldn't help noticing a script supervisor's lapse in one of the final scenes. When the invisible man—supposedly naked—is forced to flee from a burning barn, his presence is shown by *shoe*prints in the snow.

99

"My grandson, 22 years old, keeps complaining about headaches. I've told him a thousand times, 'Larry, when you get out of bed, it's feet first.' "—Henny Youngman.

When Marilyn McCuster filed a suit to become the first female coal miner in the U.S., she was in all the papers. When the Rushton mine ceiling collapsed on her, Marilyn became the first female coal miner to die on the job, joining thousands of men before her.

Human "hailstones" fell from the sky over Germany one day in 1930. A group of five glider pilots had been forced to bail out when they unexpectedly encountered a storm in the mountains. Even more unexpected was the aftermath: falling to earth, the men picked up a layer of ice in the clouds they passed through. The ice grew thicker and heavier as they fell. Despite their open parachutes, four of the five were frozen to death before they struck the ground. Perhaps even stranger, one of the "hailstones" survived.

That's a misnomer
In the sixteenth century, Spanish explorers in Mexico stopped some local Indians. The Indians asked "Yucatan?" which means "what do you want?" The name stuck!

President Benjamin Harrison was the first president to have electricity in the White House. He was so frightened of the invention he left all the lights on during the night.

Lieutenant Joseph C. Ives of the U.S. Corps of Topographical Engineers proved his worth as a prophet in 1861 when he gave us this gem: "The Grand Canyon . . . is, of course, altogether valueless. Ours has been the first, and will doubtless be the last, party of whites to visit the profitless locality."

The history of the ship *Argo Merchant* is a catalogue of disasters. In the year of 1967 alone it collided with a Japanese ship; took eight months to sail from Japan to the U.S.; suffered three fires; and was forced to make major repairs five times.

Why didn't G.M. think of this one? The president of Toyota Motors has announced the erection of a shrine in memory of all those who have died in the company's cars. The cost: about $445,-000.

101

Angry over the revocation of his pilot's license, Canadian singer Cal Cavendish revved up his plane one last time, to "bomb" the city of Calgary with a hundred pounds of pig manure.

A charmed life
That describes the experience of seaman Roy Dikkers during World War II. Sealed in a compartment when a German torpedo struck his tanker, he was freed by a second torpedo explosion. Racing on deck he found the sea around the floundering vessel ablaze with oil fires. He never had to make the fateful decision whether to stay with the sinking ship or risk the fiery sea. A third torpedo blew him far from the scene, beyond the oil slick. Landing near a floating raft, he crawled aboard and was found by a Norwegian freighter three days later.

Participants in this tale of survival still can't believe it really happened. Thrown through the steel roof of his car in a head-on collision, a Denver man landed a hundred feet away—on railroad tracks, directly in the path of a speeding train. Too late to brake before passing over the body, the engineer stopped as fast as he could and rushed back to the spot, certain he had killed the man. What he found was a guy limping, shaken, but very much alive. His only injury was the broken leg he suffered in the car collision.

Although he ultimately got used to traveling on the sea, Herman Melville, the author of *Moby Dick,* got seasick on his first ship voyage in 1839.

Goaded by the Russian Sputnik satellite, U.S. scientists and technicians rushed to develop our first entry in the space race. Accompanied by a great fanfare and press hoopla, the launch was set for December 6, 1957, at 1:44 P.M. If you had been watching on your TV you would have seen the huge rocket rise majestically to a height of three feet and explode.

Robert Todd Lincoln arrived, historically speaking, too late. On Good Friday, 1865, Robert was late returning home to the White

House. The servants told him to rush off to Ford's Theater where his parents were attending a performance. As he arrived, he watched his father Abraham Lincoln being carried away from the entrance, shot by an assassin's bullet.

In 1881 Robert Todd Lincoln had become the Secretary of War. On July 2 he was summoned to the train station by President Garfield. Lincoln arrived late and picked through a huge mob to discover Garfield had been shot.

On September 6, 1901, at the Pan American Exposition in Buffalo, New York, Lincoln was invited by the president in office at that time to attend the festivities. Lincoln arrived just after the fatal moment of the exposition when President William McKinley was shot by crazed anarchist Leon Czolgosz.

Wherever he hangs his hat is his home
Sir Joshua Reynolds painted thousands of portraits. He was bound to make one mistake. He once painted a man with a hat on his head, and a hat under his arm.

If you want to take a train in Afghanistan or Somalia, forget it. There is not a rail of track in either country.

Every high school student studies Mendelian genetics. Gregor Mendel, the pioneering biological scientist explained the laws of genetics in his experiments with pea plants. He also failed his natural science exams *twice* when he tried to become a high school science teacher.

"The right to suffer is one of the joys of a free economy."
— Howard Pyle, economic adviser to Eisenhower.

Good idea
Lloyd George of Great Britain delivered some sound advice to the Italians about picking up the sagging Italian economy. "Produce more bananas," he said, without realizing no bananas grew in Italy.

103

In Pimlico Gardens in London there is a statue dedicated to William Huskisson—the first man to be run over by a railroad train.

In 1971 General Motors recalled 6,682,084 automobiles. The left front engine mount was faulty on millions of Chevrolet automobiles and trucks. This was the largest recall in history and may be one of the great engineering blunders of modern times.

"Lincoln's mother was standing at the door of their cabin singing 'Greenland's Icy Mountain.'" Carl Sandburg wrote this line in *Abraham Lincoln—The Prairie Years.* One problem: the song "Greenland's Icy Mountain" was written 22 years after the death of President Lincoln.

Houdini was convinced that the public would never remember him as a great magician. He knew he would always be remembered as being the first aviator to cross the Australian continent in 1910.

There is a statue in Shimoda, Japan, honoring the first cow slaughtered in Japan.

In Cuzco, Peru, there is a statue of Pocahontas's father, Chief Powhatan. A foundry was supposed to ship a statue of Atahualpa, King of the Incas, but made a mistake.

The shortest war in history was not between two nations of equal power. A British ship stationed near Zanzibar entered the harbor in plain sight of Khalid Ben Bargash, the Sultan of Zanzibar. The crew of the English ship wished to watch a cricket match onshore. The Sultan declared war on Britain for invasion of Zanzibar. In 37 minutes the war was over.

On February 5, 1969, ABC television aired a comedy show called "Turn On." The show lasted one hour and was the pilot for a series to run on national T.V. It received such poor ratings the series lasted one day—February 5.

Comedian Jan Murray hosted the most unsuccessful game-show series on T.V. It was called "Meet Your Match" and ran for eight days on NBC.

In 1918 the world's first scheduled airmail flight took place. President Woodrow Wilson watched the plane take off from Washington on its way to Philadelphia on a clear spring day in May. The mail plane lost its way and landed in Waldorf, Maryland. The mail made it to Philadelphia by train.

Oliver Goldsmith, the famed English dramatist, was not a success in every field. He failed in law, the clergy, medicine, teaching, acting, clerking, proofreading, sailing, all before he wrote *The Deserted Village*, and *She Stoops to Conquer.*

Jack Carter, the second-fiddle comic, hosted a variety program in 1949 that lasted only 17 days on ABC.

ABC aired a game show series that lasted only 15 days. It was called "Bon Voyage (Treasure Quest)". The unsuccessful show ran from April 24 to May 8, 1949.

Both of James Madison's vice presidents died in office.

Famous painter Tintoretto was a superb artist and somewhat less of an historian. In his oil painting, *Israelites Gathering Manna in the Wilderness,* Moses' men have shotguns. The first gun was invented around 1300. Moses was ahead of his time, but not that much.

John Tyler was the first U.S. President to seriously be considered for impeachment.

As Secretary of State, William Jennings Bryan invited the Swiss Navy to attend the opening of the Panama Canal.

An inmate named Charles Justice helped design the first electric chair at the Ohio State Penitentiary in 1897. He was released in 1899 on parole. His name may have been ironic enough, but several years later he was convicted of murder and was electrocuted in the chair he helped design.

John Lee's executioner couldn't get it right. Lee was to be hung in 1885. The hangman couldn't get the knot right and tried three times to hang John Lee. Finally Lee's sentence was commuted to life imprisonment.

"I held onto the near edge of the landing gear and checked my balance and then hesitated a moment . . . I am the first man to wet his pants on the moon."—Edwin "Buzz" Aldrin.

An art award was given by the U.S. National Academy of Design to Edward Dickenson whose painting had been evaluated while hanging upside down.

Gorgias of Epirus was born during his mother's funeral. The mourners assumed the pregnant mother's death would cause her infant to die. Gorgias popped out of the womb while his mother was in a coffin.

Slow and steady wins the race
Tsugunobu Mitsuishi of Japan stayed stationary for 5 hours and 25 minutes on his bicycle. No one else has even come close to this mark, and for a very good reason—no one wants to try.

Deutschland Über Alles?
Not in the 1936 Olympics. Hitler wanted to prove German supremacy and Jesse Owens, American track and field star, would not let him. Owens won the 100-meter dash, long jump, 200-meter dash and the 400-meter relay. Hitler walked out, unable to watch a black American single-handedly defeat the "master race."

10

Historical Notes

Madame Tussaud, founder of the famous London Wax Works exhibits, began her successful career in jail. During the Reign of Terror in her native France she was imprisoned, and was allowed to fashion death masks of the nobles sent to the guillotine.

Footnote to history
The Pilgrims aboard the *Mayflower* didn't land at Plymouth Rock until a year after their original landing on Cape Cod in 1620. The Plymouth Rock piety was conjured up by an 18th century PR man.

Tired of the incessant quarreling of Nicias and Alcibiades, Athenian bureaucrat Hyperbolus persuaded the appropriate committee to agree to a vote on banishment for one of the two antagonists. As the vote was about to be taken, however, the opponents reached agreement; so rather than waste their preparations, the committee voted to exile Hyperbolus. He was the last citizen ostracized from Athens.

Napoleon suffered from hemorrhoids. It made it difficult for the emperor to mount his horse. According to one account, his inability to climb on his horse Nicole during the battle of Waterloo caused the great defeat of Napoleon.

In 1948, U.N. Ambassador Warren Austin spoke about peace in the Middle East. He suggested that the Jews and Arabs stop fighting "in a true Christian spirit."

The "Tyrant of Syracuse," Agathocles, died in 289 B.C. from choking on a toothpick.

Attila the Hun died in 453 A.D. during sexual intercourse.

One way or another
The wife of Claudius I tried to poison her husband with poisonous mushrooms in 54 A.D. Claudius's doctor tried to make Claudius throw up by tickling his throat with a feather. Claudius choked on the feather and died.

Alexander the Great died in 323 B.C., from a fever that he got while on a two-day orgy of women and wine.

A footnote to history
Everybody knows about the colorful ceremony staged at Promontory, Utah, when the Union Pacific and Central Pacific railroad tracks met to form the first transcontinental railroad in 1869. Well-known also is the fact that the last spike joining the rails was a golden one, driven by top officials of the two railroads. Wrong! Neither Thomas Durant of the Union Pacific nor Leland Stanford of Central Pacific could handle the 15-pound sledgehammer well enough to hit the spike. So they posed for pictures and left the golden spike to be driven by the men who had driven all the others that made the occasion possible.

Most people assume German Count Ferdinand von Zeppelin invented the type of balloon that came to bear his name. But the real originator of the dirigible was Austrian engineer David Schwartz, who succumbed to a heart attack when notified that the German government wanted to produce his design. Von Zeppelin bought the rights to the invention from Schwartz's widow.

Demosthenes, a statesman and orator of ancient Athens, was disappointed in his own self-discipline. Instead of staying home to prepare speeches, he spent a lot of his time partying. Then he struck on an ingenious way to keep himself home: he shaved one side of his head, knowing he would feel too ridiculous to go out until it grew back.

Lasting three and a half centuries, the notorious Spanish Inquisition exceeded its papal charter, anathematizing books that were acceptable to the Holy See. It went so far as to conduct heresy investigations of Saint Theresa of Avila and Saint Ignatius of Loyola, founder of the Jesuit Order.

When Sir Walter Raleigh brought seed potatoes from Virginia and planted them on his estate in Cork, Ireland, he couldn't have anticipated the consequences. Previously unknown to the Irish, the "spud" became a staple of their diet in no time. So dependent did they become on it that when a blight struck potato crops in the mid-1800s, millions of Irish people died of famine or were forced to emigrate to other lands around the world.

In Napoleon's memoirs, found at St. Helena, he firmly contended that all the battles he waged were "defensive."

Pope Calixtus III issued a decree in 1456 that Halley's comet "be entirely diverted against the Turks, the foes of the Christian name."

King Frederick of Germany fell off his horse into a puddle and drowned.

While walking to Syracuse in ancient Sicily, Aeschylus, the famed Greek playwright, paused to rest on a beach. Legend has it that an eagle carrying a turtle in his talons flew overhead. The eagle mistook Aeschylus' shiny bald head as a rock on which to drop the turtle to crack the shell. The eagle dropped the turtle and killed the poet.

114

Among her other bad features, Mary Queen of Scots was bald.

Murphy was an optimist.
There were four gasoline-powered cars in the United States in 1895. In St. Louis, two of them crashed together. Both drivers were hurt.

Don't look now
In ancient Greece women were executed if they watched just one Olympic event.

Explorer Christopher Columbus flogged members of his crew who suggested that he had reached an island. He was positive that he had discovered a new route to Asia.

The worst famine in history took place in Russia in 1914–1924. Twenty million people died during this period.

A famine in China in 1333–1337, that cost the lives of 6 million Chinese, is also believed to have been the breeding ground for the Black Plague that spread to Europe. Seventy-five million humans died during this period.

In 30 B.C. Roman leader Antony committed suicide thinking his Egyptian lover, Cleopatra, was dead. Cleopatra was very much alive, but when she found out that Antony was dead *she* committed suicide.

Alessandro Stradella, famous violinist, composer and singer, eloped with a rich senator's wife in 1682 in Venice. The senator was enraged and hired killers to murder Stradella. At one point Stradella sang to his would-be assassins and they released him. The second time it did not work; Stradella was killed.

In 1840 the East India Company of London flooded the Chinese black market with opium to make outrageous profits. The Chinese commissioner ordered the opium destroyed. Great Britain declared war. The war lasted two years and the Chinese surrendered and gave up Hong Kong in the bargain.

116

During the famous midnight ride of Paul Revere, Paul was captured by the British after turning down the wrong road and riding smack into some British soldiers.

The isolationist Fu Manchu Dynasty in China kept the famine of 1876–79 a secret. When news of the ten million deaths reached the West, the dynasty prevented relief efforts to save additional lives. All in all, 14 million people died during this period.

The captain and crew of the *Octavius* set out to find the Northwest Passage in 1762. They did not bring along enough food. The ship froze in ice at Point Barrow, Alaska. All the passengers died. Thirteen years later the ship was spotted in the Atlantic Ocean; it had drifted across the unfound Northwest Passage alone, with a crew of dead men.

"To me truth is precious . . . I should rather be right and stand alone than run with the multitude and be wrong . . . [My views have] already won for me the scorn and contempt and ridicule of some of my fellowmen. I am looked upon as being odd, strange and peculiar . . . But truth is truth and though all the world reject it and turn against me, I will cling to truth still."—Charles S. deFord defending his theory in 1931. His theory was that the earth was flat.

Jerome Bonaparte, the last descendant of Napoleon in America, died in 1945 after tripping over his dog's leash in Central Park and sustaining injuries.

In Sophocles' Greek drama, *Oedipus Rex,* Oedipus vows to punish the murderer of King Laius. Oedipus discovers that he is the murderer. Through this mistake he also discovers that he has slept with his own mother. Thereupon, Oedipus gouges out his own eyes in punishment.

Death and taxes
The Roman poet Virgil held a funeral for a housefly. In the time

of the Triumvirate no grounds that were burial sites could be taxed or parceled out as favors. The tombstone of the fly saved Virgil's property.

Adolf Hitler took a sleeping pill on the day the Allies invaded Normandy—D-Day. His aides were afraid to wake the Führer, and he slept as the Americans and British stormed the French beaches. The German generals were paralyzed without the supreme commander's orders, helping the invasion to become a success.

Marcus Licinius Crassus was the ill-fated Roman general who in 53 B.C. learned not to trust anyone. Crassus heard news of the mounting Parthian army—his enemy—and sought out a guide to tell him where to locate the Parthians. A guide was found and he led them into the Mesopotamian desert where the entire Parthian army was waiting to slaughter Crassus. Crassus and more than half his army were massacred.

Thou shalt obey . . .
Joan of Arc was accused of witchcraft and burned at the stake. Another charge raised against Joan was disobeying her parents.

11

Piety

Yuen Tong, a Buddhist monk, went into the squatting position of a long-term meditator in 1698, when he was 22. In 1760—when he was 84—Yuen died, never having changed his position. His followers embalmed the sitting saint's body and displayed it for years in Kunming's Pagoda of the Rocks.

A class act
All 78 passengers drowned when a bus plunged into a river near New Delhi, India, because members of different castes refused to share the only rescue rope.

In May of 1979 the Grand Canyon College baseball team won the Area 2, N.A.I.A. baseball championship. The members of the team celebrated with champagne. They then learned that the title had been taken away from them. The Baptist Church which owns the college forbids drinking of any alcoholic beverages.

Belgian businessmen, professional men, and even priests had been receiving pornographic letters in their mail for over a year. A police investigation turned up the unlikely perpetrator: the mother superior of a convent school. The unfortunate nun was sentenced to three months in jail.

A wealthy religious colony, located on a luxurious ranch in Mendocino County, California, benefits from a county subsidy of $63,000 a year. Colony members work the racket by signing over all their personal property to the community and then going on welfare.

The zeal of a Lancaster, Pennsylvania minister had unforseen effects: After urging his congregants to confess their sins before God and man, he was forced to listen to three females of his flock describe their sexual encounters with him.

When Moslem clergy convened in Damascus, Syria in 1933 to determine the cause of the terrible drought the area was suffering, they reached the obvious conclusion: the lack of rain could be traced to the yo-yo fad among their children. No sooner had the offending toys been taken away than the heavens opened up. Allah sent them rain the next day.

Pope Leo VIII died in 965 A.D. while committing adultery.

Mormon leader Brigham Young condemned the trousers as "fornication pants" and proscribed their use among his followers. He was talking about the new fly-front style for men, which was replacing the traditional side-buttoned flap.

Returning to his native Peruvian jungle as a missionary, converted cannibal Yumen Diaz Calderon had one slight misgiving: what if his tribesmen didn't recognize him?

From 818–855 a woman was the pope of the Catholic Church.

Pope Joan Anglicus had masqueraded as a man for most of her life. She was discovered to be a woman when she gave birth to a child.

Pope Alexander VI was the father of seven illegitimate children. He was elected to the papacy in 1492.

Pope Clement VII was an illegitimate child.

Pope John XII was so sexually active that many accused him of making the Lateran Palace into a brothel. The Pope died when a jealous husband beat him over the head in 964 A.D.

Elijah Muhammad was the prophet of the Nation of Islam, leader of the faith of Malcom X. Muhammad was involved in a sex scandal with three of his secretaries. When Malcom X learned of this he split with Muhammad. Muhammad suffered paternity suits in 1963 from his secretaries and the four children he sired illegitimately.

12

Sports

Ever hear of the Soccer War? In 1969 hostile neighbors Honduras and El Salvador were opponents in an important international soccer match. When fighting broke out among the passionate partisans at the game, it quickly resulted in declarations of war and El Salvador's army invaded Honduras, inflicting thousands of casualties. Worst of all for Honduran fans: they also lost the game.

Professional Wrestler Stanley Pinto was no match for himself one night in Providence, Rhode Island. Thrown against the ropes by his opponent, Stanley got tangled up in them. Trying to break free, he accidentally pinned his own shoulders to the mat for three seconds and was declared the loser as his opponent watched.

When the Denver Broncos suffered a 33–14 loss to the Chicago Bears in 1973, one dyed-in-the-wool Denver fan almost became dead-in-the-wool. Crushed by his team's fumbling performance, he left a despondent note, put a revolver to his head and pulled the trigger. Fortunately, according to police, he was no more successful than the Broncos and fumbled his suicide attempt.

"Half this game is 90 percent mental."—Danny Ozark, manager of the Phillies.

Billy Rohr pitched his first game for the Red Sox in 1967 and threw 8 2/3 innings without giving up a single hit. He managed only one more victory that season and was traded to Cleveland and soon retired still thinking about that last 1/3 inning in Boston.

In 1904 while batting for the Philadelphia As, Monte Cross went up to bat 503 times. He will always be remembered for his out-standingly low batting average—.182.

Curt Gowdy, who broadcasts every conceivable sports event for ABC television, spoke about the weather during a Raiders-Chargers football game in California: "Folks, this is perfect weather for today's game. Not a breath of air."

It's not easy to fill up air time with sparkling conversation. During a dreary AFL all-star game which featured a rain-soaked field, Curt Gowdy observed, "If there's a pileup there, they'll have to give some of the players artificial insemination."

Al "The Bull" Ferrara did not get his nickname for charging around the basepaths. In eight seasons with the Dodgers he never stole a base.

Never mind
In 1945, during a steeplechase race, a horse refused to make a jump so the discouraged jockey brought the horse back to the stables. The jockey was then told that all the other horses had fallen or been eliminated. The jockey took his horse, Never Mind II, back to the race and completed the course in the slowest time

ever recorded—11 minutes 28 seconds—which includes the walk to and from the stables. Never Mind II was declared the winner.

Sports fans familiar with the passionate soccer enthusiasm of Pele's countrymen will appreciate this one: In a match between the Brazilian teams of Rio Preto and Corinthians, the first goal was scored against Rio Preto within three seconds after kickoff. What made the score particularly hard for the team's fans to take was the fact that it was made while their goalie was still on one knee with head bowed, praying for victory.

Pete Gray was a real baseball hero. In 1943 he began his professional career with the Three Rivers team of the Canadian-American League. He led the league by batting .381 that year, and in 1944 he hit .333 and stole 68 bases. When he joined the St. Louis Browns in 1945 his statistics were less impressive, but he remained a favorite of the fans. Some of you may recall that the feisty little centerfielder had only one arm.

The score was tied in a baseball game between Peoria, Illinois and Port Huron, Michigan, when Dan O'Leary stepped into the batter's box for Port Huron. Elated at hitting a homer, O'Leary ran the bases backwards; third, second, first and then home. The ump signaled him out and his team went on to lose the game.

"We're all sad to see Glenn Beckert leave. Before he goes, though, I hope he stops by so we can kiss him goodbye. He's that kind of guy."—Jerry Coleman, famous baseball radio announcer, now manager of the Padres.

"It's a beautiful day for a night game."—Broadcaster Frankie Frisch.

In 1926 the Brooklyn Dodgers had a tough day on the basepaths. Bases were loaded. Babe Herman hits a single. Runner scores from third. Runner on second decides to stop at third. Runner from first rounds second, slides into third. In the confusion Babe Herman

125

rounds second and slides into third. Three runners on third. Two men tagged out. (This may be the most embarrassing play of all times: three professional baseball players piled around a single base.)

Ralph Bernstein of the Associated Press asked Philadelphia Phillies' coach Danny Ozark why he never gives a straight answer. Ozark replied, "Don't you know I'm a fascist? You know, a guy who says one thing and means another."

Dead eye
In the 1949 British Open Harry Bradshaw scored a bull's-eye. His drive contacted an upright beer bottle, smashed through the neck, and made a hole-in-one in the glass bottom. Harry kept a stiff upper lip and played through, shattering the glass and bogeying the hole.

Goalie Sam LoPresti wished he had never come to the rink on March 4, 1941. The pitiful Chicago Blackhawks' defense let the Boston Bruins take 83 shots on goal, right at poor Sam LoPresti. Sam did one hell of a job, but the Blackhawks lost the game 3–2.

A former Los Angeles Rams quarterback was arrested when he tried to sell the secret Rams playbook to the New Orleans Saints. The law officials must have been pro-football fans because they threw the case out of court. No amount of secret information could help the Saints beat the Rams, so the playbook was worthless.

Danny Ozark of the Philadelphia Phillies was asked if he had problems with the players of his losing team. "Contrary to popular belief, I have always had a wonderful repertoire with my players."

"If you can't imitate him, don't copy him."—Yogi Berra.

Ron Hunt holds a brutal major league baseball record. He holds the lifetime and season record for most times hit by a pitch—lifetime, 243, season, 50.

Luckless Mets' first baseman, "Marvelous" Marv Throneberry once hit a triple and was called out for forgetting to touch first base.

"Marvelous" Marv Throneberry had a personal black cloud hovering above him. He even admitted, "Things just sort of keep happening to me." He once chased a runner towards second base while the winning run scored from third.

The Pittsburgh Pirates couldn't wait to call up Ron Neccai from the minor leagues. They received a call from their farm club when Neccai struck-out 27 batters in one game. He was sent up to the majors, pitched very poorly, compiled a 1–6 record and retired.

Dino Restelli was touted as the new Ralph Kiner while he played for the Pirates in 1949. In his second season the "new Kiner" batted .184 and left baseball.

Only true baseball fans remember Larry Doby. He was the first black player in the American Baseball League, signing just after Jackie Robinson.

"Nobody goes there anymore; it's too crowded."—Yogi Berra.

On May 26, 1959, Harvey Haddix of the Pittsburgh Pirates was pitching against the Milwaukee Braves. He retired 36 batters in a row, 12 perfect innings. An error and one hit in the thirteenth lost Haddix the game and a chance for the record books.

"I want to thank all those who made this night necessary." —Yogi Berra during "Yogi Berra Night" in St. Louis.

The Rochester Lancers didn't want to bother the Toronto Metros of the North American Soccer League. The Lancers very politely shot only once during a game in 1975. No one else in soccer history dares to match this record.

Stay alert
The Montreal Canadiens Hockey team must have been sleeping at the opening face off against the Detroit Red Wings on January 28, 1973. Detroit's Harry Boucha took only six seconds to score against the Canadiens.

Burning rubber
Never make a wrong turn in the world's fastest automobile. Craig Breedlove got out of control in the jet-powered "Spirit of America" and left skid marks five miles long on a salt flat in Utah.

Catcher Russ Nixon (no relation to the ex-president) played 12 years in professional baseball and never stole one base. Pitchers would not even offer him the courtesy of holding him on first.

In 1954 Karl Spooner was a very hot pitcher for the Dodgers. He pitched back-to-back shutouts in Brooklyn and in the two games struck out 27 batters. He contracted arm problems and never pitched again after 1955.

Stay in the black
Paul Runyan, the P.G.A.'s leading money-winner in 1934, won $6,767 in tournament play. His travelling expenses that year totaled $6,765. Profit = $2.00.

In 1964, the Philadelphia Phillies led the National League by 6½ games with one week of play left in the season. When seven days had past they found themselves in a tie for second place with the Cincinnati Reds. Many Phillies fans still carry World Series tickets that were printed anticipating a Philadelphia pennant. (Dr.

Benjamin Kendall, a noted Philadelphia physician, drove to Connie Mack stadium to make sure the Phillies were not playing in any World Series games.)

Marathonist Kokichi Tsuburaya of Japan was a perfectionist. He won the bronze medal in the 1964 Olympics and promptly committed suicide, feeling he had let down his country.

The "A-Mazing Mets" had a rough time of it in 1962, their first season. Two starting pitchers *lost* 20 games each, a reliever lost 16 in a row, and a catcher named Chris Cannizzaro (who Casey Stengel called "a defensive catcher who can't catch the ball") dropped even the good pitches the staff managed to throw.

Speak softly and carry a big stick.
The 17th hole at North Carolina's beautiful Black Mountain Golf Club is 745 yards long. It is rated at a par 6 but it is not unusual for golfers to score double-digits reaching the the green.

In 1975 Topps Chewing Gum Company held a contest among major league baseball players to determine who could blow the biggest bubble-gum bubble. The winner was Kurt Bevacqua of the Milwaukee Brewers. Unfortunately for Kurt and for Topps, the company did not think Kurt Bevacqua was going to make the major leagues that season and there was no baseball card issued with his picture.

In the World Series of 1947, Joe DiMaggio made what seemed to be a game-winning hit. It was stolen from him by a man named Al Gionfriddo. The catch will go down as one of the most exciting in baseball history. It was also a memorable one for Gionfriddo because it was his last major league catch.

"I usually take a two hour nap, from one o'clock to four." —Yogi Berra.

129

Only one horse spoiled a perfect record for Man o'War. It happened in 1919–20. The horse's name was "UPSET."

That's how the cookie crumbles
Payne Rose holds a special distinction in the manual of the American Bowling Congress. In September 1962, Payne bowled six 7–10 splits in a row.

Every New York fan cringes when he thinks of the 1962 Mets baseball team. The Mets went 40–120 in their first season and finished 60½ games behind the league-leading San Francisco Giants.

Philadelphia's baseball teams have finished in last place 41 times.

"You observe a lot by watching." —Yogi Berra.

George Blanda was the oldest active football player ever to play in the National Football League. He aged a great deal during the 1962 football season when he was quarterbacking the Houston Oilers. He threw 42 interceptions that year.

"If people don't want to come to the ballpark, how are you going to stop them?" —Yogi Berra.

"Anybody who can't tell the difference between a ball hitting wood and a ball hitting concrete must be blind." —Yogi Berra.

In his only World Series performance, Ted Williams batted .200 and could not muster one extra base hit.

Jim Nash was a pitcher in the National Baseball League who at the age of 20, in his rookie season, pitched 12 wins with only one loss. He returned for his second season in 1967 overweight and with a sore arm. He lasted only part of that season.

130

Who me?
In 1964–65 Bailey Howell broke a dubious record in NBA basketball history. He committed 345 personal fouls in one season.

That's how the cookie crumbles
Payne Rose holds a special distinction in the manual of the American Bowling Congress. In September 1962, Payne bowled six 7–10 splits in a row.

Every New York fan cringes when he thinks of the 1962 Mets baseball team. The Mets went 40–120 in their first season and finished 60½ games behind the league-leading San Francisco Giants.

Philadelphia's baseball teams have finished in last place 41 times.

George Blanda was the oldest active football player ever to play in the National Football League. He aged a great deal during the 1962 football season when he was quarterbacking the Houston Oilers. He threw 42 interceptions that year.

"If people don't want to come to the ballpark, how are you going to stop them?" —Yogi Berra.

"Anybody who can't tell the difference between a ball hitting wood and a ball hitting concrete must be blind." —Yogi Berra.

In his only World Series performance, Ted Williams batted .200 and could not muster one extra base hit.

Jim Nash was a pitcher in the National Baseball League who at the age of 20, in his rookie season, pitched 12 wins with only one loss. He returned for his second season in 1967 overweight and with a sore arm. He lasted only part of that season.

131

In 1928–29 the luckless Chicago Blackhawks of the National Hockey League did not manage to score one goal per game and thereby recorded the lowest goal-per-game average in history—.75. They were the only team to sink below the average of one goal per game.

The combined ERA of the 1930 Philadelphia Phillies pitching staff was 6.71. This is the absolute, rock-bottom worst pitching statistic of any major league team—ever.

John Breen, the former manager of the Houston Oilers football team, was asked why his team was performing so poorly: "We were tipping off our plays. Whenever we broke from the huddle, three backs were laughing and one was pale as a ghost."

In 1895 Mike Grady of the New York Giants baseball team lost his concentration on one play. Third baseman Grady fielded an easy grounder and muffed it; his throw missed the first baseman entirely; when the runner rounded second, the first baseman threw back to Grady who dropped it, and when Grady finally recovered the ball and threw home, the ball flew over the catcher's head into the stands—four errors in one play.

Former pro quarterback George Mira hates playing on Astroturf. During a football game he fell on the artificial surface and cut his finger very severely—on a zipper holding the field together.

Duke Snider, the Brooklyn Dodgers slugger, hit only .143 in his first World Series.

Long and foul
On September 3, 1906, Joe Gans of the United States fought Oscar "Battling" Nelson of Denmark at Goldfield, Nevada for the light-

weight title. The fight lasted a long time— he 42 rounds. The referee insisted Nelson fouled Gans and the American was declared the winner.

"He slides into second with a standup double."—Jerry Coleman, radio announcer.

After the Philadelphia Phillies had lost a 15½ game lead in their division by dropping ten games in a row, coach Danny Ozark waxed philosophical: "Even Napoleon had his Watergate."

In the 1953 World Series, awesome switch-hitter Mickey Mantle of the Yankees struck out five times and totaled a .208 average.

Ridin' high in April, and cut down in May
Manolete, the greatest bullfighter of all time, dominated bull fighting for 12 years until 1947 when he was gored by a charging bull.

Danny Ozark had these words to say about the Philadephia Phillies infielder Mike Andrews: "His limitations are limitless."

Everyone knows pitchers are not supposed to be hitters. Milwaukee pitcher Bob Buhl proved the rule to the highest degree. In 1972 Buhl went hitless in 70 trips to the plate.

"It's not over until it's over."—Yogi Berra.

The Tennessee Friendsville Academy basketball team had trouble getting a winning momentum going for some time. From 1967 to 1973 the Academy lost 138 straight games.

During the U.S. Open Golf Championships in 1938, Ray Ainsley teed up on the par 4 16th hole. His ball landed in a brook. Nineteen strokes later he pushed on to the 17th hole.

133

Marv Throneberry, Mets' first baseman, made so many errors in his career that Mets Stadium began selling T-shirts with VRAM spelled across the chest. VRAM is MARV backwards.

Philadephia Phillies' general manager Paul Owens began traveling with the luckless Phillies and many people thought coach Danny Ozark might lose his job. Ozark said that Owens was "not intimidating and, furthermore, I will not be cohorsed."

Don Drysdale, one of the great pitchers for the Los Angeles Dodgers in the National Baseball League, holds a very vicious record. He hit 154 batters with his pitches.

"It gets late early out there."—Yogi Berra speaking of the shadows in Yankee Stadium.

George McBride, a Washington shortstop, was at bat more than 1,000 times during his career. He retired with a .218 batting average. That's a record—for lowness.

The longest boxing match in history (not under modern rules) took place over two days. Andy Bowen and Jack Burke fought for 110 rounds in New Orleans. Unfortunately neither man won, the fight was called no contest.

Casey Stengel, colorful Mets' manager, was so afraid of the "A-Mazing" Mets making horrible mistakes that he once had Charlie Neal run around the bases twice after a home run to insure that Neal had touched all the bases.

In the 1966 World Series, Dodger outfielder Willie Davis committed three errors.

"Marvelous" Marv Throneberry of the Mets made many errors, but the fans still adored him. An Italian restaurant had a Marv Throneberry night, and the affair was so crowded Marv could not get in the door and was forced to eat elsewhere.

In 1915 Skeeter Shelton was called up to play for the New York Yankees. Skeeter was a fast runner but could only exhibit it running to and from his fielding position in the outfield. In his only major league season he went 1 for 40 at the plate and retired with a lifetime batting average of .025.

"There's a fly ball deep to center field. Winfield is going back, back, ... he hits his head against the wall. It's rolling towards second base."—Jerry Coleman, radio announcer.

Look at them now
The Philadelphia 76ers is one of the most powerful teams in professional basketball. In 1972–73 they lost 73 games, the worst ever in NBA history.

"And now the pretty little girls will press among you with their little cans. Please give till it hurts."—Harry Balough, fight announcer, doing a promotion for the March of Dimes at Madison Square Garden.

Someone told Yogi Berra that Ernest Hemingway was a great writer. Berra replied, "Yeah, for what paper?"

In 1962 the "A-Mazing Mets" ended their dismal season by hitting into a triple play. Casey Stengel was asked about his thoughts on the '63 season: "We've got to learn to stay out of triple plays."

Few people know that Anna Kemenes, a Hungarian, is one of the world's great gymnasts. You might recognize her by the name that the Romanian government has forced her to use as a member of an ethnic minority: Nadia Comaneci.

A reporter asked Don Larsen this question after Larsen pitched a perfect game in 1956: "Is that the best game you ever pitched?"

In 1974 the basketball team of Englewood Cliffs College knew they were going to have a rough time beating Essex County College. But they didn't expect to lose 210–67—a record for collegiate play.

"On the mound is Randy Jones, the left-hander with the Karl Marx hairdo."—Jerry Coleman, radio announcer.

Nice guys finish last.
The Phillies' Robin Roberts was a very good National League pitcher. He refused to brush batters back with pitches in order to move them away from the plate. The hitters found out. One season he gave up 46 home runs; in his career 502 balls left the park. Both of these are records for a pitcher.

Asked if the losing Philadelphia Phillies had a morale problem, manager Danny Ozark said, "This team's morality is no factor."

"Rich Folkers is throwing up in the bullpen."—Jerry Coleman, sports announcer.

Bob Feller, the great Cleveland pitcher, played in the World Series only once and lost both games he pitched. He had waited 10 years to reach the Series.

In 1974 Los Angeles Laker Center Elmore Smith went to the foul line and shot in a 3-to-make-2 situation. Smith missed the rim, backboard, and net on all three shots.

What Don Meineke lacked in talent he made up for in aggressiveness. Don played basketball for the NBA's Fort Wayne Pistons during the 1967–68 season. He fouled out of 26 games that year.

After being congratulated by the press for out-foxing another manager, Danny Ozark of the Philadelphia Phillies replied: "Who knows what evil lurks in the hearts of men except the Shadow?"

137

The Chicago Black Hawks of the National Hockey League were shut out of eight consecutive games during the season of 1928–29. They established a league record.

The Houston Astros traded Rusty Staub for Donn Clendenon. Clendenon never reported to play and Staub became a great star for the Montreal Expos.

Boston manager Dick O'Connell of the Sox traded Sparky Lyle for Danny Cater. Lyle won the Cy Young award for pitching the next year with the Yankees. How many of you have heard of Danny Cater?

"Old Diz knows the King's English. And not only that. I also know the Queen is English."—Dizzy Dean, pitcher and sports announcer.

Reggie Jackson is the flamboyant home run king of the New York Yankees of the American League. He is also the easiest man to strike out in the history of baseball.

Rusty Staub was traded from the Mets to Detroit for pitcher Mickey Lolich. Lolich had one uneventful season, Staub hit home runs all over Detroit.

The Soviet news agency, Tass, reported a new sport in Russia— grenade-throwing. In 1976, 36 million Russians participated in flinging de-activated grenades in a competition which resulted in the nationwide finals in Tashkent. Valentina Bykova, a 39 year old woman, threw her pineapple 132.8 ft. Good throw, comrade.

For some unknown reason the Mets traded fastballer Nolan Ryan to California for fat and aging Jim Fregosi. Nolan Ryan continued to be the best pitcher in the majors while Fregosi continued to eat.

Wally Pipp, first baseman for the Yankees, was sidelined one day with a headache. As a replacement the Yankees started a young

138

player named Lou Gehrig. Lou played a few more games after that —2,130 more—in a row. Wally never got off the bench.

In 1916 the Georgia Tech football team beat Cumberland University by a score of 222–0. Cumberland's defeat was the worst suffered by any team in history. Famous sportswriter Grantland Rice watched the game and surmised that Cumberland's best play of the game "came in the third quarter when halfback George Allen skirted left end for a thirty yard loss."

On October 21, 1956, the Chicago Bears played the Baltimore Colts. The Colts' quarterback, Shaw, dropped back for a pass and three huge defensemen of Chicago blitzed. They pounced on Shaw and inadvertently broke the Colts' quarterback's leg. The Colts had no alternative, they had to put in their substitute quarterback, a young man who had been cut by Pittsburgh the year before. His name was Johnny Unitas. It seemed that Shaw's leg never fully recovered.

What's the shortest distance between two points? No one knew the answer to the question in the football game between Chillicothe and the Texas All-Stars. A Chillicothe man fumbled on the three yard line, the ball skipped into the end zone where a Texas defensive back fielded the ball and ran towards his end zone across the length of the field. As he neared the goal line he fumbled and a Chillicothe player picked up the football and ran back 90 yards. He was tackled on the four yard line, a loss of one yard on the play.

A young player for the Daytona Beach Islanders baseball team was a teriffic pitcher and outfielder. The coach couldn't decide where to put him. A spill in the outfield sprained his shoulder and ruined his pitching career. Stan Musial had to concentrate on becoming a hitter.

Pete Reiser of the Brooklyn Dodgers had no "object constancy." Each time he ran back for a ball in the outfield he would forget that there was a wall bordering the field. He led the National

139

League in batting as a rookie but never reached his full potential because he kept slamming into the outfield walls.

Bobby Thomson of the Milwaukee Braves broke his ankle in spring training in 1954. He was to be sidelined for part of the season. The Braves' management was forced to dip into their farm club to find a replacement outfielder. In their Savannah club they found a man named Henry Aaron. Hank kept hitting home runs until he hit more than anyone else. Bobby's ankle is still hurting.

A promising young pitcher named Herb Score was hit in the face by a line drive. He had led the American League in strikeouts and had won 36 games in two years. After the blow to the face he never recovered, winning only 17 games in his last five seasons.

A hunting accident sidelined shortstop Charley Gelbert. The St. Louis Cardinals had to find a replacement and they found Leo Durocher. He was one of the leaders of the famous Gas-House Gang in 1933.

Eddie Waitkus was playing well for the Philadelphia Phillies in 1949. A psychotic female fan shot him in the stomach almost midway through the season. He recovered from the wound and helped the Phillies in 1950 to win the pennant. He was careful about his friends afterwards.

Max Baer was so confident of winning the world heavyweight title against James J. Braddock in 1935 that he wasn't really concentrating. Although a 10–1, Baer lost the fight and Braddock was nicknamed the "Cinderella man."

Muhammad Ali can dance like a butterfly and sting like a bee but in 1978 his overconfidence and lack of training caused him to lose to an inexperienced Leon Spinks.

In a publicity stunt in 1931, Joe Sprinz caught a baseball dropped out of a blimp hovering 800 feet above the ground. The gutsy catcher broke his jaw when he caught the ball.

Pity the poor catcher who caught against the Washington American League team in 1915. During one game Washington runners stole 8 bases in one inning.

Davey Moore fought Sugar Ramos to defend the featherweight championship of the world in 1963. Moore lost the title and his life.

Ted Horn finished in every place but first place in the Indianapolis 500. He died in a crash during a race in Illinois without ever winning racing's biggest race.

Baseball ain't what it used to be
The old Philadelphia Athletics once played a double-header against two teams. These two teams, Williamsport and Danville, are perhaps the greatest losers ever in baseball. They lost by scores of 101–8 and 160–11 respectively.

"Gee, for a fat girl you don't sweat much." —Football star Alex Karras to a girl at an Iowa State dance.

Foul ball
In 1940 a third baseman named Bert Haas waited for a ball to roll foul across the third baseline. It didn't. Runners were scoring. Quick-thinking Haas got down on hands and knees and blew the ball out of bounds with his breath. The umps ruled in his favor.

Until 1980 the Philadelphia Phillies had never won a single World Series.

Limousines for the feet
Detroit Piston center Bob Lanier has problems buying socks. He wears a size 22 sneaker.

In a famous crew race on the Thames, Cambridge's oarsmen defeated Oxford's crew by the largest margin in history. The Oxford shell sank minutes after the race began. The six oarsmen rowed until they were entirely underwater.

The Mets should learn never to trade anyone. It seems every player they trade away becomes a superstar. This was the case when the Mets sent Amos Otis to Kansas City for a man named Joe Foy. Otis played in almost every All-Star game since that time, and Foy . . . well, rumor has it that he's a real nice guy.

In 1925 Babe Ruth complained of a bellyache. Sportswriter W. O. McGeehan called it "the bellyache heard around the world." After his ailment the Babe never played the same and the Yankees dropped to seventh place by the end of 1925.

Bobo Holloman got off to a great start as a rookie. In his first trip to the mound he pitched a no-hitter. He completed only one other game in his major league career and was soon out of baseball.

In the 1937 All-Star Game, Dizzy Dean broke his toe when a line drive hit by Earl Averill smashed into his foot on the pitcher's mound. In the next three years, the great fastballer could not recover from the injury and he won only 16 more games.

From 1947–53 St. Paul's Poly in Virginia lost 41 games in a row in football. During one stretch of their streak they were outscored 890–0.

The San Francisco Giants traded George Foster for Frank Duffy. Foster went to the Cincinnati Reds to lead the National League in home runs. Duffy enjoyed the view from the bridge.

That's no bull.
Forty-two major world matadors have been gored to death by their horned opponents.

The 1919–20 Quebec Bulldogs make everyone else in National Hockey League history look great. In just 24 games, 177 shots slammed into the Bulldogs' goal. That's a record.

When a coach hires a pro-quarterback he assumes that the man he hires can hold onto the football. Well, famous NFL quarterback Dan Pastorini fumbled 17 times during 1973 and Roman Gabriel of the Rams fumbled 105 times during his career—both National Football League records for bad hands.

"Young Frank Pastore may have just pitched the biggest victory of 1979, maybe the biggest victory of the year."—Jerry Coleman, announcer for the San Diego Padres.

Ralph Walton was adjusting his mouthpiece in his fighter's corner when the bell rang to start the first round of his 1946 boxing match against Al Couture—10½ seconds later Ralph Walton was knocked out by Couture.

The old Chicago Cardinals of the NFL lost 29 consecutive games from 1942–45.

In 1918 a row of stands collapsed at the Hong Kong Jockey Club and a fire ignited—604 people were killed. According to the Guiness Book of World Records this was the worst disaster in modern sporting event history. In ancient Rome, the upper tier of the Circus Maximus collapsed and 1100 people watching a gladiator event were killed.

During the Desert Classic golf tournament in Palm Springs, Bob Hope was speaking to a beautiful young female scorekeeper on national television. He asked her, "How old are you?" "Twenty-four," she answered. "I've got balls older than that," Hope replied. "Oh—I mean *golf* balls."

"Grubb goes back, back . . . he's under the warning track, and he makes the play."—Jerry Coleman, sports announcer.

Sports' announcer Bob Neal was watching his home team, the Cleveland Indians, play the Oakland Athletics. Charlie Finley, the flamboyant owner of the Athletics, had decided to hire ball girls, instead of ball boys, to retrieve the foul balls. Bob Neal observed, "It appears that Mr. Finley has decided to let girls chase the boys' balls instead of boys chasing boys' . . . "

Ralph Branca would like to call back one pitch that he threw. It was during the 1951 playoff game against the New York Giants. Branca was pitching for the Dodgers in a tie game and threw a bad pitch to Bobby Thomson. October 21st will always be remembered as the day Bobby Thomson hit the home run and won the pennant, while Branca will be remembered as the goat. (Famous Irish diner owner Brian O'Rourke was born on this same day while his father was weeping for the Dodgers.)

In 1977 Harvey Gartley fought Dennis Culette in a Golden Gloves boxing competition. Gartley was counted out in a knock-out 47 seconds after the opening bell. Culette never made contact with Gartley. The young Gartley was so excited during the match that he "danced himself into exhaustion and fell to the canvas"— knocking himself out and losing the fight.

"Next up for the Cardinals is Barry, Carry, . . . Garry Templeton."—Jerry Coleman, baseball radio announcer.

"A nickel ain't worth a dime anymore."—Yogi Berra.

Cassius Clay (before he became Mohammad Ali) knocked out Sonny Liston in one minute fifty-seven seconds in their fight in Lewiston, Maine.

Baseball coach Yogi Berra on appearance: "So I'm ugly. So what? I never saw anyone hit with his face."

Yousouf Ishmaelo was the colorful Turkish wrestler who insisted on carrying his wealth in gold coins strapped to his belt. While on a sea voyage, his boat began to sink, and Ishmaelo refused to take off his money belt and drowned.

145

"If [Pete] Rose's streak was still intact, with that single to left, the fans would be throwing babies out of the upper deck."—Jerry Coleman, radio sports announcer.

Ross Cleverley knocked out D. Emerson with one punch in New Zealand in 1952. The entire bout lasted seven seconds.

One step forward, two steps back.
In 1967 the Denver Broncos of the NFL played the Oakland Raiders and gained a grand total of –5 yards with their running game. This negative rushing attack was the worst in NFL history.

"Bob Davis is wearing his hair differently this year—short and with curls—like Randy Jones wears. I think you call it a frisbee." —Jerry Coleman, radio sports announcer.

"Hrabosky looks fierce in that Fu Manchu haircut."—Jerry Coleman, sports announcer.

Teddy Martinez, shortstop for the "A-Mazing" Mets, made five errors in one game, a typical Met performance. "I can't play perfect every day," Martinez declared.

World champion flyweight boxer Pascual Perez may have eluded opponents because they could not find him. He weighed only 107 lbs. and was 4 feet 11 inches tall.

The Washington Redskins couldn't get their offense moving on December 6, 1940—ironically, one year before Pearl Harbor, another debacle. The Bears beat the Redskins 73–0 and won the NFL championship.

Jon Hardy of the Chicago Cardinals of the old NFL had a problem picking out his receivers during one game in 1950. He found several men willing to catch the ball on the other team, however, and threw eight interceptions.

146

One of the most "successful" matadors of all time, Juan Belmonte, was speared 50 times by angry opponents.

"Hendrick simply lost that sun-blown pop-up."—Jerry Coleman, colorful sports announcer.

"Bill Dickey learned me all his experiences."—Yogi Berra.

Yogi Berra's wife, Carmen, told him she had seen *Doctor Zhivago*. Yogi asked, "Oh, what's a'matter with you now?"

"Hello, Fred Hoey everybody speaking."—Fred Hoey, Red Sox broadcaster in the 30s.

In Biarritz, France, a town not noted for its golf, Chevalier von Cittern played a round of 18 holes. His hook was acting up worse than ever before; he shot a 316, 244 over par.

During the 1974 season the Washington Capitals of the National Hockey League went 8–67–5. This is the worst season of any modern hockey team.

"Homer hit a Foxx."—Fred Hoey, very excited as he broadcasted a Red Sox game with Jimmy Foxx at bat.

At one time the mistake-plagued Mets had two pitchers named Bob Miller. Casey Stengel called one Nelson. Bob Miller, the left-hander, commented about playing for the Mets, "I got tired of ducking line drives and backing up home plate."

The Cleveland Browns of the NFL were once penalized 209 yards in one game.

"Let us reflect back nostalgically on the past."—Howard Cosell.

The Greek soccer fans are serious. Soccer referee Stavros Rammos was out on the field doing his job but no one seemed to appreciate him. After the game one irate fan bit off Rammos' ear.

Spanish bullfighter, El Cano, died in 1852, but not in the ring. He had an argument with his wife while he was in the hospital. As he stood to strike her, he had a hemorrhage and promptly died.

"The doctors X-rayed my head and found nothing."—Dizzy Dean, pitcher and sports broadcaster.

Sportscaster Chris Schenkel sometimes gets emotional during a football game—"The forward pass was caught by a New York Giants receiver . . . with an excellent maneuver he got by a Washington defender . . . he faked him right out of his jocks! . . . (silence) . . . and his shoes as well!"

Jim Dorey of the Toronto Maple Leafs was in a bad mood one day in a game against the Pittsburgh Penguins. He committed nine penalties for a total of 48 minutes in the penalty box. He must have been very upset during the second period; the referees charged him with seven penalties.

Tommy Warren knocked down Jack Havlin 42 times in a fight in 1888.

Pool hall great, Minnesota Fats, contracted a lung disease from inhaling blue dust from cue-tip chalk.

That's why they call him "Bonehead." In 1908 the Chicago Cubs met the New York Giants. The score was tied 2–2 in the last of the ninth with two out and Giants runners on first and third. The Giants got a single, and the runner scored from third. Fred Merkle, the runner on first, seeing the game was won, ran for the clubhouse. Famous Chicago second baseman, Johnny Evers, took the ball and tagged second base. The umpire ruled Merkle out for not following through on his base running. The Cubs won the game and the win forced a playoff later in the season. The Giants lost and Fred Merkle's error earned him the nickname "Bonehead Merkle."

Give me a break.
Art Morin of Massachusetts, bowled 22 spares in 30 frames, but not one strike. His three game total was 465.

Clarence Mitchell of the Dodgers should not have even stood up to bat during the World Series of 1920. His line drive was caught by Cleveland second baseman Bill Wambsganss. There were men on first and second and both had started to run. Wambsganss stepped on second and tagged the runner coming from first—an unassisted triple play.

In the 1908 Olympics, Italy's Dorando Pietri led the 26-mile marathon and lumbered into the stadium after a long, grueling race. As he ran the final lap in the stadium, he ran the wrong direction and then collapsed as he tried to correct his mistake. Several judges helped him to his feet and he finished the race. Unfortunately the victory went to American John Hayes. Pietri was disqualified for receiving assistance.

Sportscaster on radio—"DiMaggio is back, back, back to the wall, his heads hits it, it drops to the ground, he picks it up and throws it to third."

Dizzy Dean was once criticized for his lack of good syntax. Dean asked, "Sin tax? What will those fellers in Washington think of next?"

Two Eskimo football teams in King Island, Alaska, were antici-pating their annual New Year's Day Ice Bowl Game. A large ice field near the village was picked as the practice site because of the flat, smooth surface. As they walked outside for their practice, the Eskimos noticed their field had drifted away.

"He's dead at the present time."—Casey Stengel, manager of the Yankees.

Dan O'Leary was called out after hitting his first home run—he had run the bases in the wrong direction. O'Leary played for Port Huron in the early days of baseball.

In 1933 John Tarleton College lost to San Antonio Junior College in basketball by the slim margin of 27–26. Tarleton then won 86 consecutive games, carrying them into the season of 1938 when they played San Antonio and again lost by a score of 27–26.

"He was originally born in Tennessee."—Curt Gowdy, during a sports' broadcast.

In 1847, famous Spanish Matador Jose de los Santos ran away from a charging bull and leapt over the protective fence in the ring for safety. As he fell over the fence, Santos gored himself with his own sword.

Babe Herman of the Dodgers once stole second base with the bases loaded.

Juan Anillo, a Spanish bullfighter, died while watching a bullfight. A fellow spectator hit him over the head with a bottle during an argument in 1925.

Easy does it
A correspondence chess match between Dr. Munro MacLennan and Lawrence Grant of Scotland started on November 24, 1926. It is still in progress.

Tommy Henrich was up at bat for the Yankees in the 1941 World Series. The Brooklyn Dodgers were ahead 4–3 in the ninth inning. Henrich took two strikes. The Dodgers had never won a world championship and they were now one strike away. Hugh Casey threw a strike and the game seemed to be over. Catcher Mickey Owen tipped the ball and it passed by him. Henrich ran to first and the Yankees rallied to win the game. Owen's flub cost the Dodgers the Series.

In 1900 in the National Baseball League, the Reds traded Christy Mathews for Amos Rusie. Mathews went on to win 367 games. Rusie never won again.

In 1938 the Chicago Bears of the National Football League couldn't seem to get their claws into the ball. They fumbled 56 times, a season record.

In Russia in 1931 Wasyl Bezbordny and Michalko Goniusz slapped each other's faces for 30 hours. Face-slapping was a sport in Kiev at the time. The match was a draw.

Missed it by that much
Steve Stevenson had rolled eleven strikes in a row. He needed one more to bowl a perfect three hundred game. He crossed the foul line on the bowling lane and blew his last frame—final score 290.

Billy Conn almost achieved the greatest upset in heavyweight boxing history. He had been defeating the great Joe Louis for twelve rounds, but was so excited by the prospect of the title and beating the "unbeatable Louis" he lost his concentration and was knocked out in the unlucky 13th round.

Alone again, naturally
Larry Breer of Kipp High, Kansas, had to hold up more than his end of a bargain. All of his teammates fouled out of a basketball game against Aurora High. Breer had to play alone, five on one. Kipp High only lost by two points.

151

In the 1800s Oxford's chess team suffered a tremendous loss. They had been carrying on a correspondence match with another chess team and were soundly defeated by them. The team was from the famous Bedlam Insane Asylum.

Jack Dempsey wanted to avenge his loss to Gene Tunney in 1926. They met in 1927 in Soldier Field in Chicago. Dempsey demolished Tunney. He then crowded over Tunney while the referee tried to wave him to a neutral corner. Dempsey was so tenacious he refused to budge from over Tunney. The referee did not start the count on Tunney until Dempsey would move. Tunney rose and cleared his head. He went on to beat Dempsey in one of the most exciting fights in history. All Dempsey had to do was take three or four steps.

During a Chicago Bears-Los Angeles Rams football game, a sideline official flipped a down marker by mistake changing the down from second to third. Not one team player, coach or fan noticed the error. Eighty thousand people attended the game.

Jerry West and Elgin Baylor are two of the greatest basketball players ever to play in the National Basketball Association. They are on everyone's top ten players list. Ironically, although they reached the playoffs seven times and the finals four times, they never won a championship for the Lakers while playing together.

During a Boston-Baltimore game in 1894, a fight broke out between third baseman John McGraw and Boston's Tom "Foghorn" Tucker. Both teams crowded the field as the brawl exploded. The irate fans also participated and one particularly angry man in the bleachers set fire to the ballpark and started one of the largest fires in Boston which destroyed 170 buildings.

In the 1929 Rose Bowl Game, center Roy Riegels of California picked up a Georgia Tech fumble and started running for the Georgia Tech goal line. He got confused and ran 75 yards in the wrong direction before his teammates stopped him. Georgia Tech scored a safety because of the error and Riegels' mistake lost the game for California.

Jack Doyle, a heavyweight boxer who was nicknamed the "Irish Thrush," wound up for a big punch in the second round against

153

Eddie Phillips. Doyle threw the big right and missed Phillips. The force of his windup carried Doyle head first through the ropes and into the arena. He knocked himself out during his fall and the "Irish Thrush" heard birds calling as he was counted out.

During the 1954 Cotton Bowl, Rice halfback Dicky Moegle started running down field for a 95-yard touchdown. Alabama fullback Tommy Lewis watched the play developing on the Alabama bench. Midway through Moegle's run, Lewis hopped off the bench and tackled Moegle. Then Lewis quickly shot back to the bench as if nothing had happened. The referee was not to be fooled and awarded the touchdown to Rice. Despite Lewis' overenthusiasm, Alabama won the game.

Every one interested in baseball knows that Bob Gibson had the lowest Earned Run Average for a single season as a pitcher. There are 11 men in baseball history who really can appreciate how difficult a feat Gibson performed. These eleven men have the distinction of acquiring "infinite earned run averages" which is achieved by a pitcher who yields one or more home runs without ever retiring a single batter during his career. For some unknown reason, two of them, Elmer "Doc" Harmann of the Cleveland Indians and Fred Bruckbauer of the Minnesota Twins, were both born in New Ulm, Minnesota. Ironically, these are the only two major leaguers to hail from New Ulm.

Bad timing
The St. Louis Blues of the National Hockey League did not know what hit them on November 22, 1972. They were playing the Pittsburgh Penguins and in one two minute period five goals in a row were scored against the blue Blues.

In 1935 an enraged Dartmouth fan ran into the line of scrimmage during the Dartmouth-Princeton Ivy League Championship. The unidentified man lined up with the Dartmouth players and yelled "Kill those Princeton guys." He then leapt across the line of scrimmage only to be beaten up by the entire Princeton squad. Doctors carried off the mysterious fan.

154

The 1946 World Series between the St. Louis Cardinals and the Boston Red Sox was all tied up in the last of seven games. Enos Slaughter was the runner on first for the Cardinals when a single was hit to center field. Red Sox shortstop, Johnny Pesky, took a relay throw from the outfield and expected Slaughter to hold at second base. Pesky took his time and held onto the ball while Slaughter raced towards third and rounded for home. Pesky threw home but it was far too late and the Red Sox lost the World Series by one run.

In Derby, England, a soccer player was fined ten shillings for smiling at the referee.

Watch your step
Mountain climber Christopher Timms once fell down a steep ice floe on Mt. Elie de Beaumont into a crevasse and his climbing companion was killed—they both had fallen 7,500 feet. Timms survived, however, and set a record that no one envies, the longest fall ever survived.

That old black magic
Obare Asiko, commissioner of the Kenya Football Association, had to issue a stern warning. Asiko spoke out against all the practicing witch doctors in Kenya who were casting spells during the soccer games. "The practice of witchcraft is unsettling our efforts to clean up soccer."

Achille's heel
Joe DiMaggio missed 65 games in 1949 because of a bone spur in his heel. When he returned he had a superlative season. But two years later in 1951 the heel problem forced him to retire with many good seasons yet to play.

Dave Nicholson was a promising bonus-baby for the Baltimore Orioles in 1959. His best year was 1963 when he hit 22 home runs, but he had some trouble keeping his eye on the ball; in 1,419 at-bats he had 573 strike-outs.

155

The 1975–76 Kansas City Scouts hockey team had a record of 12–56–12. In their last 44 National Hockey League games, they won a total of 1 game.

Bob "Hurricane" Hazle fizzled out after just two months in the National Baseball League. He came up from the minors to the Milwaukee Braves in 1957 and batted .403 in 41 games. In 1958 he batted .179, was traded to the Tigers where he batted .241, was released, and then retired.

Clyde Vollmer will always remember one month in 1951. He was playing for the Boston Red Sox in the National Baseball League and in July he won 13 games with his batting skill. He was then traded to Washington who needed some hitting, and Vollmer only managed to bat .256. He retired in 1954, waiting for another July.

A bull market
In 1884, a Spanish matador named Romano killed 18 bulls in one day in Seville. That is a record for bullfighters to be proud of, but not bulls.

In 1939 un-beaten, un-tied, un-scored upon Duke played USC in the Rose Bowl. In a fluke play in the last minute of the game a third-string quarterback named Doyle Nave threw a pass for USC and scored a touchdown in one of the biggest upsets in college football.

"Those amateur umpires are certainly flexing their fangs tonight."
—Jerry Coleman, poetic baseball radio announcer.

Soccer fans in Italy once forced a soccer referee's car off the road and into a ditch after he fled from the stadium. Apparently the referee had made some questionable calls.

Pitching great Dizzy Dean became a sportscaster after he retired from baseball. He was known for his colorful speech: "The score is tied, and the runners on second and third are taking a lead off their respectable bases. There goes the runner . . . he slud into third base!"

"How can I hit and think at the same time?"—Yogi Berra.

When Washington State played San Jose State in a football game in 1955 the temperature was zero degrees, but a stiff wind made the mercury drop even farther. One person attended the game.

The Philadelphia Quakers in the National Hockey League in 1930 went 15 straight games without scoring a point.

It was bad enough when the Chicago Bears trounced the Washington Redskins by a score of 73–0 in 1940, but to add insult to injury, the Bears had kicked so many extra points, the referees had run out of footballs!

"They're off and rocking at Runningham."—Fred Hoey, sports broadcaster.

Jim Marshall of the Minnesota Vikings scooped up a fumble and ran 66 yards into the end zone—the wrong one. The San Francisco 49ers scored a safety. Luckily, Marshall tried to compensate for his mistake and helped the Vikings win the game.

In 1933 a football team was formed in Cincinnati called the Reds. They scored three touchdowns all season. Twelve years before, a Cincinnati team called the Celts lost 8 out of 8 regular season games. Both teams lasted one year.

League bowler Richard Caplette of Connecticut had a very bad day on Sept. 7, 1971. He started the game inauspiciously by rolling a three. Things went downhill from there; he rolled 19 gutter balls and finished the game with a whopping score of 3.

Bad call
A Greek referee of a soccer match had to disguise himself as a priest to escape a hostile stadium of fans. The irate spectators found out his scheme and pelted him with rotten fruit.

Dave Schultz of the Philadelphia Flyers is a hard-nosed hockey player. It's almost amazing that he finds time to play the sport. He spent eight hours in the penalty box in 1974–75.

The drivers are not the only ones who have a tough time at the Indianapolis 500. The 300,000 fans dump approximately 6.6 million pounds of trash in the stadium each year.

Dartmouth played Cornell in a 1940 football game. A referee made a confused call in the last nine seconds of the game. Red Friesell, the referee, forgot what down it was and ruled that the ball should remain with Cornell, when in fact Cornell had used its four downs. In the final seconds of the game Cornell scored a touchdown to win. Friesell admitted his mistake after watching films of the game. Cornell coach Carl Snavely conceded the game to Dartmouth based on Friesell's error.

Clem McCarthy, track announcer, listed the winner of the 1947 Preakness to a huge national radio audience. He announced Faultless the victor, when, in fact, Jet Pilot had won. Faultless indeed!

The Dallas Tornados of the North American Soccer League won 2 games in 1968 and lost 26. It was rough going. During their 22 game losing streak, 109 goals were scored against them.

Louis Fox took billiards very seriously. A fly landed on a ball he was shooting at during a match in 1865. He missed, lost the match and committed suicide.

Having an important husband in the bowling world could not help Pat Crowe of Miami, Florida. Her husband was president of the Women's International Bowling Congress but Pat still managed to bowl five consecutive 8–10 splits.

You only live once
The famous Cleveland Indians shortstop, Ray Chapman, worked

twice as hard as everyone else one day in 1920. He was up twice, got two hits (both doubles), stole two bases, scored two runs, made two put outs, and made two assists. He was also hit twice by bad pitches; and second throw killed him.

Don't bother standing
"Battling" Nelson fought Christy Williams in 1902. In 17 rounds, Williams was knocked down 42 times.

The Mets are full of "a–mazing" stories. In 1969, in their triumphant World Series appearance, Al Weis batted .455. Al Weis had been a reserve all year but seemed to come alive and played an important role in the Series victory. In 1970 Weis played in 11 games and was released by the Mets.

Sometimes Bobo Newsom forgot what uniform to put on. Bobo was a major league pitcher who sometimes touched base with the Washington Senators when he was not being traded. Bobo was traded 16 times in his career and had the distinction of leading the American League in losses four times.

Pitcher Clay Kirby had a no-hitter going but lost the game because his manager called in a pinch-hitter for Kirby, and the opposing team scored off the reliever.

In the final stretch of the 1957 Kentucky Derby, world-famous jockey, Willie Shoemaker, misjudged the finish line and sat up in his saddle of Gallant Man as if he had won the race. Iron Liege pulled up alongside Gallant Man and won by a nose just as Shoemaker discovered his mistake.

Baseball fans will remember that in 1932 a Red Sox player named Dale Alexander tore up the league and won the batting crown, hitting .367. Two years later Dale Alexander left baseball, a virtual unknown.

In 1969 the naughty Oakland Raiders of the NFL were penalized 1,274 yards during the season. That's almost a mile of penalties. It's also a single-season record.

A fanatic Pennsylvania woman golfer had a tough time on the 16th hole at the Shawnee-on-Delaware course in 1912. Her first shot went into the Binniekill River and started rushing downstream. She hopped into a boat and found the ball 1½ miles downstream. She continued the hole and finally sank a beautiful putt and scored a 166. The hole was a par three.

Another brilliant career cut short
Midget Eddie Gaedel stepped up to bat for the St. Louis Browns who were playing the Detroit Tigers in 1951. He walked on four pitches, his strike zone being the size of a piece of toast. On his jersey he wore the number "⅛." The next day he was ruled out of the league.

I get a kick out of you
The Welsh have a sport ironically named "purring." Two men face each other, each holding the shoulders of his opponent. They kick each other's shins until one man loses his grip on his opponent. To add to the pain, their shoes are reinforced. The sport has failed to catch on in other nations.

13

The Printed Word

I can get it wholesale
The editors of the Cambridge Bible found a mistake in the Bible's translation. The famous "coat of many colors" worn by Joseph was actually a mis-translation of "a long garment with sleeves."

When he had finished drafting the text of his book, *The French Revolution,* Thomas Carlyle sent it to his scholarly friend John Stuart Mill for criticism. Mill's maid, in his master's absence, mistook the manuscript for scrap paper and used it to light a fire. Carlyle started the entire volume over from scratch.

The wisest of all newspapers, *The New York Times,* once lambasted Professor Robert Goddard for asserting that rockets could fly in a vacuum. "He seems only to lack the knowledge ladled out daily in high schools." When Apollo 11 was lauched in July, 1969, the *Times* wrote, "It is now definitely established that a rocket can function in a vacuum. The *Times* regrets its error."

The best-selling American book ever (over 100 million copies sold) was authored by Noah Webster. If you're thinking it's his dictionary, you're wrong! It was his blue-backed *Speller,* published in 1783.

During a writing career spanning eighteen years, seven novels, eight other full-length books and innumerable articles, Australian William Gold received a total of about 50 American cents—for an article accepted by a Canberra newspaper. None of his other works were ever published.

"A deep armchair stood before the fireplace. She took it up between thumb and forefinger, handling it delicately, set it down on the other side, and considered it profoundly."—U.S. author Fanny Heaslip. (*Wild Goose Chase,* 1929.)

During his presidency, Woodrow Wilson was the victim of a printing error. A journalist, reporting on one of Wilson's nights at the theater, meant to write, "Wilson spent most of his time entertaining Mrs. Galt." When the newspaper was printed the line read, "Wilson spent most of his time entering Mrs. Galt."

Karl Marx did not lack confidence. He once boasted to Friedrich Engels that he would complete *Das Kapital* in five weeks. Fifteen years later his masterpiece was published.

Before the John Day Company accepted Pearl Buck's novel, "The Good Earth" for publication, it had been rejected by fourteen publishers.

Overcome with grief at his wife's death in 1862, English poet Dante Gabriel Rossetti buried an unpublished manuscript of some love sonnets in her coffin. His wife was out of sight, but apparently the sonnets weren't out of Rossetti's mind; he had her coffin exhumed some time later to recover them. In 1870, the poems were published.

English newspaper reporter W. T. Stead, researching an article on the evils of prostitution during the Victorian era, kept a 13-year-old girl in a brothel. He was arrested and imprisoned for his journalistic dedication.

In 1889 the *Literary Digest* shared this gem of wisdom with its readers: "The ordinary 'horseless carriage' is a luxury for the wealthy; it will never, of course, come into such common use as the bicycle."

Every college student is armed with the popular writing manual "The Elements of Style" by William Strunk, Jr. and E. B. White. It has become the standard English textbook. Here is a sentence that got by the authors: "The subject of a sentence and the principal verb should not, as a rule, be separated by a phrase or clause that can be transferred to the beginning."

In Nikolai Gogol's famous short story, "The Nose," collegiate assessor Kovalyov discovers that he has lost his nose.

Akaki Akakievich, hero of Nikolai Gogol's "The Overcoat," loses his overcoat at a party of petty officials and spends the rest of the story searching for it. Without the warmth of his coat he dies of pneumonia.

The famous remark, "Let them eat cake," was thought to have been said by Marie Antoinette. Actually the famous line appeared in Rousseau's *Confessions* when Marie was only 12 years old and living in another part of Europe.

In 1977, Chuck Ross, a freelance writer was frustrated with receiving rejection slips from publishers. He re-typed a novel by Jerzy Kosinski called *Steps*—a novel that had won Kosinski the National Book Award. Ross sent the manuscript to 14 publishers and 13 literary agents. All 27 rejected the book.

"One morning Gregor Samsa awoke and discovered he was a cockroach."—opening line of Kafka's "Metamorphosis."

"I resolved if possible, to get to the ship; so I pulled off my clothes, for the weather was hot to extremity, and took to the water ... I found the ship's provisions were dry; and being well disposed to eat, I went to the bread room and filled my pockets with biscuits."
—mistake found in *Robinson Crusoe* by Daniel Defoe.

Apparently A. Conan Doyle never read his own work after he finished writing. Doctor Watson's leg injury in the *Sign of Four* moves to his shoulder in *A Study in Scarlet.*

"His right arm has been amputated at the shoulder and the sleeve on that side hangs flabbily. Then he goes over to the table and sits down, resting his elbows, his chin in his hands, staring somberly before him."—Eugene O'Neill (stage direction in *Where the Cross Is Made*)

In Guayaquil, Ecuador, there is a statue commemorating poet Jose Olmedo. The statue is actually a likeness of Lord Byron which was bought second hand; the town could not afford to commission a real likeness of Olmedo.

The Miami Herald reported on the tough obscenity laws in Ft. Lauderdale, Florida. The new laws ban obscenities in books, movies, magazines and records for those under 17. In the ordinance, the obscenities that are banned are listed so graphically that the ordinance itself could not be read by anyone under 17.

Virginia Graham, on her show, "Girl Talk," was plugging an author's work: "Once you put down one of her books, you can't pick it up again."

Victor Hugo ordered his servant to steal his clothes so that he would be at his desk naked. Unable to go out of doors, he would *have* to work on his manuscript *Les Miserables.*

169

"It was a scene never to be forgotten when Roosevelt, before the Chief Justice of the Supreme Court and a few witnesses, took his simple bath." New York newspaper in 1940.

Bret Harte, the famed short story writer, made this oversight while writing about the death of a highly respected citizen in California. "She was distinguished for her chastity above all the other ladies in this town." Of course Harte meant charity, so while proofreading the story he noted the change with a question mark. In the next issue of the paper the line read as follows: "She was distinguished for her chastity? above all the other ladies in this town."

14

Winners?

Another of Senator Proxmire's Golden Fleece Awards: the Department of the Interior for spending $145,000 to install a wave-making machine in a Salt Lake City swimming pool.

Another "Golden Fleece Award": the Pentagon spent $3000 for a six-month test to see whether carrying umbrellas detracted from the appearance of military officers.

Two thousand five hundred dollars was alloted to Arlington County, Virginia for a study on why people are rude to each other on public tennis courts. The grant was provided by the National Council for the Humanities. . . . (If you are wondering where half your paycheck goes every week.)

A Golden Fleece Award from Senator Proxmire went to the Department of Education for spending $21,592 of our money to teach college students how to watch television.

In 1980, the Mass Transit Authority purchased 660 Flxible Grumman buses from the Grumman Corporation on Long Island for use in New York City. In 1981 all 660 buses were recalled by Grumman because of serious cracks and structural damage to the buses. One bus with a full load of passengers cracked in half in Queens. Luckily no one was hurt. A Grumman spokesman blamed "the bad condition of New York City streets," for the broken chassis of the buses.

A Golden Fleece Award from Senator Proxmire went to the National Endowment for the Arts for sponsoring a $2500 study to find out why tennis players try to hog the courts.

One of Senator William Proxmire's Golden Fleece Awards went to NASA for giving the contract to pick up radio signals from outer space to one firm for $15 million when another company had bid only $6.5 million.

Senator Proxmire's "Golden Fleece Awards" include one to the Department of Agriculture for a two-year, $90,000 study of the behavioral determinants of vegetarianism.

Senator William Proxmire of Wisconsin, originator of the "Golden Fleece" awards for wasteful government spending, once had the tables turned on him. A conservative organization spotlighted Proxmire's own efforts to have the Department of Agriculture fund a research center to study dairy forage—in other words, the stuff cows eat. The multimillion dollar project would have been established, coincidentally, at the University of Wisconsin.

The National Science Foundation received one of Senator Proxmire's Golden Fleece Awards for their $36,000 study of Himalayan mountaineering. Someone in the bureaucracy must have goofed, however, because the Foundation's request for an additional $14,576 was denied.

A Golden Fleece Award with an oak leaf cluster went to the National Institute of Mental Health for funding a $97,000 study by two University of Washington professors of a whorehouse in Peru. The academics staunchly defended their grant, pointing out that the brothel investigation was only one of more than a dozen they conducted among Peruvian mountain tribes. Senator Proxmire took the match, however, when he published this quotation from the brothel report: "By visiting the brothel at various times, it was possible to obtain a good idea of its everyday functioning."

175

Year-end splurges are a favorite way for bureaucrats to waste public money, according to Senator Proxmire, originator of the Golden Fleece Awards. If any agency is found to have money left over at the end of the fiscal year in September, its next year's allocation may be cut, a fate worse than death. The Senator's 1980 winner in this category was Clark Air Force Base in the Philippines, where they managed to get rid of their leftover $715,000 in no time.

Senator Proxmire gave one of his Golden Fleece Awards to the National Highway Traffic Safety Administration, which paid $120,126 to develop a motorcycle that could steer backwards. No one could handle the bizarre vehicle.

Even great legislators make mistakes
"Property must not be taken without compensation, but . . . some property may be taken or destroyed for public use without paying for it, if you do not take too much."—Oliver Wendell Holmes. Springer v. Government of Phillipine Islands, (1928).

The Federal Aviation Administration once spent $57,800 to study the measurements of airline stewardesses.

The Law Enforcement Assistance Administration once spent $27,000 to find out why inmates want to escape from prison.

The U.S. Post Office once spent 4 million dollars promoting the use of the mails, despite the fact that the U.S. Post Office runs at an incredible deficit. Senator William Proxmire issued a Golden Fleece award for wasteful spending to the Post Office.

"If your miracle shade tree doesn't grow up to roof-high size or more the first season—up to sixty feet by maturity—if it doesn't soar higher than even the magnificent winged elm, taller than even the stately mountain ash, wider than even the most majestic pop-

176

lar ... then simply return the tree and your money will be refunded—no questions asked."

—Capital Nurseries Sales Co.

Department of Housing and Urban Development and Economic Development Administration (HUD & EDA) spent $279,000 on a community center in an area where a community didn't exist. It was built in the woods in a remote part of Michigan. The center collapsed in 1979 and no one knew about it for days. Senator William Proxmire gave this project a Golden Fleece award for wasting public money.

15

The Hunt

Pan American Airlines security personnel were concerned about the theft of miniature bottles of liquor used to serve drinks in flight. To trap the thieves they rigged a clock device to the door of the liquor cabinet of one of their planes. The idea was to record the times when the cabinet was opened, to help determine whether ground crews were involved in the thefts; but when a stewardess discovered the device, a bomb alert was put into effect. The flight was rerouted to Berlin, where the passengers were hastily evacuated from the 727 by emergency exits. Pan Am spokesmen put the cost of the unscheduled landing at about $15,000. The tiny bottles of booze cost the airline about 35 cents each.

An ice fisherman in Edwardsburg, Michigan hauled a four-pound beauty out of the lake, cleanly removed the hook from the mackerel's mouth and placed the fish on the ice to re-bait his line. The thrashing mackerel flung itself in the air, locked its teeth on the fisherman's leg and had to be pried loose by two men. The bite required a doctor's attention.

All tourists in National Parks delight in seeing the "cute fuzzy bears." The brown bear is perhaps the most dangerous man-eater on earth.

Reformed cannibal tribesmen in Papua, New Guinea expressed a willingness to return to their traditional man-eating ways if it would help attract tourists to their area. Too civilized to attack and kill their ancient tribal enemies any longer, they offered to use corpses from the morgue for the tourist shows.

When skyjacking became epidemic at American airports in the early 1970s, airlines hired psychiatrists to develop a profile of the typical skyjacker. One company put two shrinks on duty to spot likely suspects at an especially busy eastern terminal. The operation was so secret that the two new security men were unaware of each other's existence. You guessed it: within a day one of them had arrested the other as a skyjacker type.

A prolific hunter, the second Marquess of Ripon was credited with shooting more than half a million birds during his life. On the day of his death, in 1923, he downed 52 grouse that morning.

An Arizona hunter accidentally shot himself in the leg. Trying to get attention from fellow hunters nearby, he fired his gun again —and hit himself in the other leg.

Good hunting
U.S. drivers kill more game animals than all U.S. hunters combined.

16

Royalty

In one of the shortest reigns in history, King Louis XIX led France for 15 minutes.

George, Duke of Clarence, died in 1478 when his brother Richard III drowned him in a wine vat.

James Douglas, the Earl of Morton, died in 1518 when he was beheaded by a "guillotine". Douglas had brought the device to Scotland to maintain justice.

Henry I of England died after gorging himself on lampreys.

In Anthony Vandyke's portrait of Charles I of England he mistakenly painted Charles holding two gloves—each for the right hand.

Count Stenbock, an English nobleman, died when he fell into his own fireplace during a drunken harangue in 1895.

Alexander, King of Greece, died in 1920 of blood poisoning. It seems he was bitten by his pet monkey.

Anne Boleyn had lots of problems. A marriage to the ruthless Henry VIII was one of them. Having six fingers on one hand was another. Not bearing a son was her last.

Philip VI of France got angry at his own troops during the battle of Crecy in 1346. When Philip's first line of attack failed, the men retreated. Philip had his own men cut down with arrows as they ran to safety. At the end of the battle Philip had lost 4000 men and the enemy—the English—had only 100 casualties.

Harsh Persian Emperor, Nadir Shah, was shot by his own body-guard in 1747.

Egyptian princess Cleopatra married two of her own brothers. For several generations her family had been involved in brother-sister marriages. Cleopatra was her own sister-in-law, and her mother was her aunt.

George I, King of England, couldn't participate in the deliberations of his ministers. Heir to Britain's throne by virtue of his descent from James I, his majesty was German by birth and language. Less interested in the British Empire than in his little German principalities, he never bothered to learn English.

Fulk Fitzwarine IV of England died in 1135 as his horse entered a swamp. Fitzwarine drowned in his heavy armor. He was retreating from the disastrous Battle of Lewes.

Warned by a fortune teller that he would die of alcohol, Duke Antonio Ferdinando of Guastella, Italy, swore off drinking for life. He kept his oath, but the sinister prophecy was still fulfilled. Somehow a bottle of rubbing alcohol he was using to massage himself caught fire and burned him to death.

In 1500 B.C. the Kauravas and Pandavas clans shared control of an Indian kingdom, but the Pandavas were wealthier and the Kauravas resented their superiority. So Sakuni Kauravas challenged Yudi Pandavas to gamble for the entire kingdom. Yudi's pride as head of the Pandavas clan wouldn't permit him to ignore the challenge, so he proceeded to lose his slaves and his personal fortune on successive tosses of the dice. Unable to quit, he gambled away his brothers' wealth, the kingdom, his personal freedom, and finally his beautiful wife Draupade. He never caught on that Sakuni's dice were loaded.

In 1890 Emperor Menelik of Ethiopia sent to the U.S. for three of the new electric chairs we had started using to execute criminals. His Imperial Majesty had overlooked one detail, however: there was no electric power in his country. To avoid its being a total loss he used one of the hot seats for a throne.

Like many other rulers in the 16th century, Margaret of Austria took precautions against death by poisoning. She drank only from a goblet made of pure rock crystal, because it was thought that this rare material revealed the presence of poison. When a clumsy servant dropped the goblet one day, a minuscule fragment of the crystal found its way into Margaret's shoe and was imbedded in her foot. Unnoticed at first, the splinter soon caused a massive, painful infection. Surgeons, summoned far too late, attempted to amputate the foot, but Margaret died, poisoned by her "protective" crystal.

It was a rather sticky situation. The Duke of Monmouth, an illegitimate son of English monarch Charles II, had been gruesomely executed and his remains buried, when courtiers realized no official portrait of the fellow existed. So the body was promptly exhumed, the head sewn back on, and the corpse propped up to "pose" for a hasty, anonymously-painted likeness.

185

Peter the Great was one of Russia's most autocratic rulers. Probably no incident of his reign revealed his temperament more fully than that involving one of his mistresses, a lady named Hamilton. Discovering that the beautiful woman had another lover, he had her beheaded. As a cautionary exhibit for future mistresses, he displayed the preserved head of Mrs. Hamilton in his bedroom.

Another sartorial note: The sleeve buttons on men's jackets began with a practical purpose. To break his soldiers of the nasty habit of wiping their noses on their tunics, Emperor Frederick the Great of Prussia had the buttons cast and sewn on the men's sleeves.

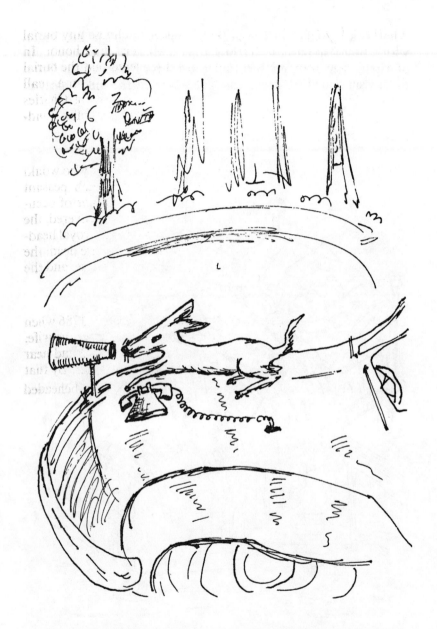

In one of his fleets of luxury cars, King Farouk of Egypt had a
horn that made the sound of a dog being run over.

Charles I of England allowed Ben Johnson to choose any burial place he wanted in Westminster Abbey—a very high honor. In 1637 Johnson died, and King Charles I discovered that the burial plot Johnson had chosen had already been used, except for a small square about a foot and a half across. Inventive King Charles solved the problem by burying the famous writer in a coffin standing straight up.

An ancient tradition threatened death to any impostor who would place the royal crown of Bohemia on his head. Such peasant superstitions didn't frighten the Nazi military governor of occupied Czechoslovakia. When the hidden crown was discovered, the Kommandant promptly crowned himself and tried the royal headgear on his two sons. Within a short time, all three were dead: the father by a patriot's bullet; one son by a fall from a horse; and the other in combat.

The Marquis de Pelier was a cocky young nobleman in 1786 when he was thrown in jail for whistling at Louis XVI's gorgeous wife, Marie Antoinette. Half a century later, when he was 72 and near death, someone thought to release the forgotten prisoner. By that time Marie Antoinette had been dead for 43 years—beheaded during the French Revolution.

17

Scientific Statements

Another "expert" heard from
Dr. Dionysius Lardner, a professor at University College, London, in the 1800s—informed the world that travel by steam-powered trains "... is not possible, because passengers, unable to breathe, would die of asphyxia."

So much for the English
Dispatched by Parliament in 1878 to report on the status of Tom Edison's light bulb experiments, an English observer told his countrymen: "Edison's ideas are good enough for our transatlantic friends, but unworthy of the attention of practical or scientific men."

Francis Bacon died in 1626 while doing an experiment to see if snow delayed the decay of dead bodies. He caught cold and died.

1902 was a prime year for expert predictions:

1. *Harper's Weekly*—"The actual building of roads devoted to motor cars is not for the near future, in spite of the many rumors to that effect."

2. Simon Newcomb, astronomer—"Flight by machines heavier than air is unpractical and insignificant, if not utterly impossible."

Flash!
"The world . . . in its general decadence bears adequate witness that it is approaching its end. There is less rain in winter to encourage the growth of seeds; springtime is not now so enjoyable or autumn so fruitful; the quarries, as if from weariness give less stone and marble, and the gold and silver mines are already worked out . . . Everything in these days is rushing to its doom." These were the fears of Cyprian of Carthage, 250 A.D.

H. G. Wells blew it on this one in 1902: "I must confess that my imagination, in spite even of spurring, refuses to see any sort of submarine doing anything but suffocating its crew and floundering at sea." Less than fifteen years later German U-boats were the scourge of Allied shipping.

In a reflective mood, Albert Einstein looked back at his life—"If I had only known, I would have been a locksmith."

In 1962, during the flight of Mariner I, a computer programmer forgot a hyphen when programming the rocket's course and the Mariner veered off course and was lost. This hyphen-loss cost the NASA program 18.5 million dollars.

One of the "Sleeping Prophet" Edgar Cayce's most famous predictions concerned the breaking off of California and its disappearance into the Pacific. Cayce never gave a precise date for the disaster, but his followers concluded from his cryptic sayings that the date would be April, 1969. When the recalcitrant state refused to depart on schedule, some hasty recalculations showed the error: it would happen in 1975, the faithful said. The latest version prophesies the disappearance in 1982.

If you're looking for a quick and easy two-credit college course, consider Southeast Missouri State University's offering: a one-week seminar with UFO expert Harley Rutledge plus a kit of materials to help you identify unidentified flying objects scientifically.

For years plant scientist Dr. Robert Foster worked to cross a cucumber with a canteloupe at his University of Arizona labs. The object was to produce a pickling cucumber that would take to the desert climate as well as a canteloupe. In 1976 Foster thought he had created a successful hybrid, but his "pickeloupe" was all seeds in its center. The story ended happily, however: Foster has since produced a vegetable that has the flesh of a cucumber without seeds.

Philosopher-mathematician Blaise Pascal once locked himself in his room for several days when he was a child. When he finally unlocked his door, his distraught family learned that the little genius had worked out all the theories of Euclidean geometry without knowing them.

In 1913 inventor Lee de Forest, originator of the radio audio tube, was tried for fraud because he had promised investors that it would soon be possible to transmit the human voice across the Atlantic.

Ernst Mach was a famous physicist at the University of Vienna. From his work we have learned a great deal about inertia and mechanics. He said "I can accept the theory of relativity as little as I can accept the existence of atoms and other such dogma."

Nikola Tesla was one of the most important physicists in the modern age. He did insist, however, that atomic power was a joke, and that the power in the atom could not be unlocked by man.

Dr. Dionysius Lardner, a British professor at University College in London, stated that if a railway train achieved a high speed like 120 miles per hour, the passengers would be unable to breathe.

193

Ernest Rutherford was essential to the modern study of nuclear physics. He was one of the first teachers of nuclear science. In 1933, however, he claimed that the power of the atom could not be unleashed.

"I cannot imagine any condition which could cause this ship to flounder. I cannot conceive of any vital disaster happening to this vessel. Modern shipbuilding has gone beyond that." —E. J. Smith, captain of the Titanic.

Dr. Dionysius Lardner, a professor at University College in London, stated in 1830 that a steamship would never be able to cross the Atlantic because it would require more coal than the ship could hold.

The famous lightning experiment of Benjamin Franklin consisted of tying a key to a kite to attract electricity. The experiment "attracted" a lot of public attention and many imitators tried their luck with the kite and key. The next two men who tried died of electrocution.

"The demonstration that no possible combination of known substances, known forms of machinery, and known forms of force, can be united in a practical machine by which men shall fly long distances through the air, seems to the writer as complete as it is possible for the demonstration of any physical fact to be." — Simon Newcomb, American astronomer, in 1906. Apparently he had not heard about Orville and Wilbur Wright's flight at Kitty Hawk in 1903.

Galileo Galilei perfected the telescope and advanced astronomy many years. He also spent too much time looking at the sun and went blind in his last years.

Famed scientist Aristotle was not always correct. He claimed that heavier objects fell faster than lighter objects.

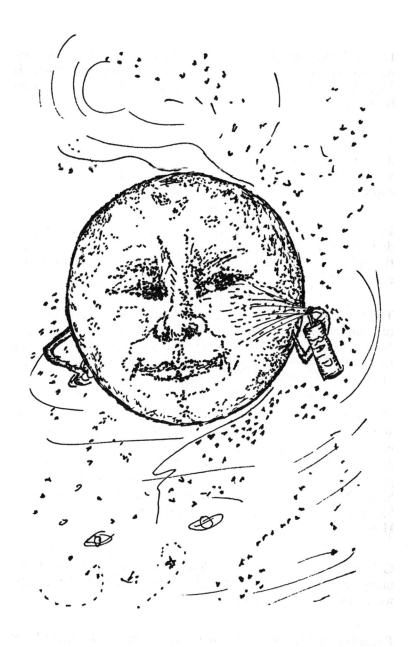

Astronomer William Pickering in 1924 offered the theory that the dark spots on the moon were caused by huge swarms of insects.

Oh yeah?
According to U.S. Rear Admiral Clark Woodward in 1930, "So far as sinking a ship with a bomb is concerned, you just can't do it."

Aristotle claimed that the heart, and not the brain, was the center of sense and intelligence in the human body.

Aristotle believed that forms of life could be created without any type of evolutionary process. He thought insects sprang from the mud, and maggots crawled out of dead meat.

Scientist and artist Leonardo Da Vinci made some mistakes. He believed that a falling object's speed increases by the distance it covers, when in actuality it is the time elapsed.

World famous astronomer Simon Newcomb made many important contributions to the study of the heavens. He did state, however, that flight by machines heavier than air was impossible.

In 1897 Lord Kelvin, a British scientist who invented the Kelvin Theory of Thermodynamics, stated that the Earth could not have been inhabited for more than 20 million years even though there was much evidence at the time to disprove him.

18

Believe It or Not

Zeuxis, a Greek painter in the 5th century B.C., died while laughing at a funny painting he had done.

Teddy Roosevelt's wife and mother died on the same day.

Why was Ignatz von Roll, a German turkey farmer, putting tiny fezzes on all his gobblers? It seems he was fascinated by the connection between "turkey" and "Turkey," and he was convinced that the birds should look like citizens of that country. If he kept the headgear on them, Ignatz reasoned, after a while he would get baby turkeys born with fezzes on.

In 1975 Joseph Figlock was walking in Detroit and a baby fell fourteen stories out of a building and landed on him. One year later history repeated itself. Figlock was walking by the same building and another baby fell from above. Both babies and Figlock are still alive.

In 1979, a Spanish Air Force jet was participating in a target practice run near a hillside in Spain. The gunfire of the jet ricocheted off the mountain and blew up the plane.

Many things have gotten their names by mistake. When Captain Cook asked the natives of the Endeavor River tribe what a strange animal that rushed past him was called, they replied: "Kangaroo." In the Australian aboriginal language, "Kangaroo" means "I don't know."

Gerard De Nerval was a romantic writer who died in 1855. He committed suicide in an odd manner—he hung himself with an apron string strung from a lamp-post in Paris.

Freedom means different things to different people. John Adams and Thomas Jefferson both died on July 4, 1826; James Monroe died five years later on July 4, 1831.

It's hard to believe what you read in a medical journal. In the November 4, 1874 issue of American Medical Weekly, the strangest case imaginable was described. During the Battle of Raymond a soldier was shot in the scrotum. The same bullet that struck the soldier pierced the abdomen of a 17-year old girl—278 days later the girl gave birth to a baby. A doctor removed a lead pellet from the baby, proving the unbelievable story. The soldier was told that his sperm was carried on a flying bullet and impregnated a young girl. The stunned soldier visited the girl, and eventually they married. Talk about a case of hit or miss!

In Poland, "Polish jokes" are told about the Ukrainians.

Enough said
The suicide rate among psychiatrists is six times that of the general population.

Alexander Hamilton was an illegitimate child.

In 1932 Russia suffered a famine that killed 5 million people. Two mistakes caused the lack of food: a governmental error, and a popular error. The government exported too much wheat, and the peasants slaughtered half of the Russian livestock to protest farm prices. Because of these actions there was no bread or meat for Russian tables from 1932–34.

The famous American song "Home on the Range" contains the lyric "where the deer and the antelope play." There are no antelope on this continent—only pronghorn sheep.

The comic strip character "Superman" was created by two teenagers from Cleveland. After dozens of newspaper comic strip editors turned down the "Superman" idea as improbable and ridiculous, they sold all the rights for the "Man of Steel" for a total of $130.

Most Americans would assume that Smith or Jones is the most common family name in the world. The most common, however, is the name Chen.

The duck-billed platypus has been called a freak of nature. It is a mammal but the females do not have teats; the young are fed through holes in the mother's abdomen. A prominent zoologist, after studying the animal for a prolonged period, exclaimed,

"That thing is just one big mistake."

There are more than 200,000 railroad grade crossings in the United States. Only about 50,000 have gates or warning devices of any kind.

If you poured ten gallons of water into a ten-gallon hat, you would ruin the hat, and the floor. The hat was named not for its ability to hold ten gallons of liquid, but because of a mistake in a translation from Spanish. The "galon" was the braided trim on Mexican sombreros.

Bobby Walthour might be called the Rasputin of bicycle racing in terms of his survival ability. His list of injuries include: left collarbone (broken 18 times), right collarbone (broken 28 times), legs (46 stitches), face (69 stitches), ribs (broken 32 times), fingers (8 broken), declared fatally injured (6 times) and declared dead (twice!).

Famous painter Salvador Dali was expelled from a Madrid art school when he was a boy.

You can't keep a good man down
In 1916 Prince Yusupov and other Russian aristocrats decided that the powerful healer, Grigori Rasputin, should die. They laced his wine and cakes with heavy doses of cyanide. Rasputin gorged himself on the meal, eating as if he were an army of men. Prince Yusupov was shocked that the poison did not affect Rasputin. He drew his pistol and fired at Rasputin. Yusupov was even more surprised when five bullets failed to kill Rasputin. Finally the treacherous healer was thrown into a burlap sack and tossed into the river to drown.

Birds such as the chickadee and dove can "throw" their voices to trick predators. Mockingbirds can deceive humans with their ventriloquism, but not other birds.

The clubhouse at the Sodom and Gomorrah Golfing Society was 1,250 feet below sea level near the Dead Sea in Israel. The clubhouse burned down in 1948. The course was not used after the fire. Golfers found the temperature "hot as hell."

Permaflex Ltd. of England exports oil to Arab nations—for lighter fluid.

You have to be in good shape to bowl in Tokyo World Lanes Bowling Center in Japan. It may take "hours" to walk to your lane; there are 252 of them.

Crocodiles have nothing to fear but themselves. They are the true kings of the jungle, having no known predators—except other crocodiles. When food is scarce, crocodiles will eat each other.

If you stick a stock of liquor in your locker,
It is slick to stick a lock upon your stock,
Or some joker who is slicker's going to trick you of your liquor,
If you fail to lock your liquor with a lock.
(Five times as fast)

204

Linda Morgan was a passenger on the ill-fated *Andrea Doria* which collided with the *Stockholm* in 1956. After the *Andrea Doria* sank Linda Morgan was found alive on the *Stockholm*.

The fine quality camel's hair brushes are made out of squirrel hair. They were mistakenly called camel's hair because of the English mispronunciation of the brushes' German inventor—Herr Keml.

"I wake up at 5 A.M. some mornings and hear the planes coming in at National Airport and I think they are bombing me."— President Lyndon Johnson.

J. David Stern, the former publisher of the *New York Post*, was famed for his forgetfulness. A journalist met Stern on the street and asked him to lunch. Stern agreed and they sat down to eat. "Funny, I'm not a bit hungry," Stern told the waiter. "Why should you be, sir," the waiter replied. "You just had lunch here five minutes ago."

In 1922 Max Flack of the Chicago Cubs and Cliff Heathcote of the St. Louis Cardinals were traded for each other. This is not unusual except that they were traded after the first game of a double-header between the two teams and during the second game both men played in different uniforms.

The Toltecs, a Mexican Indian civilization, went to war with wooden swords. They did not want to seriously injure their enemies.

State mineral of Mississippi: Iron pyrite (fool's gold).

The Premier Drum Company of England once sold tom-toms to Nigeria.

In Enterprise, Alabama, there is a statue commemorating the boll weevil. The plague of the cotton-eating insects forced farmers to plant other crops and helped the farms grow.

America is the land of opportunity, but according to the Federal Trade Commission, 9 out of 10 new businesses fail in the first year.

Erik Erikson, the famous psychoanalyst, flunked one of his Harvard psychology courses. ´

A British company, Associated Health Foods of Godalming, actually sells pasta to Italy. (Whole wheat of course.)

In 1152 Louis VII king of France shaved off his beard, angering his wife Eleanor, who divorced him. She married Henry II of England and a war began between France and England that lasted 301 years.

Lightning strikes again
In 1933 in Tanganyika, Africa,—now Tanzania,—four elephants were marching in a line connected by their trunks. A single bolt of lightning killed all four elephants.

It's tough being single. Five times as many males are stutterers than females.

Why me?
Besides man, the only other creature that contracts leprosy is— the armadillo.

Petr Ilich Tchaikovsky received bad reviews on his last symphony, the Symphony no. 6 in B Minor. Tchaikovsky purposely drank a glass of unboiled water, contracted cholera and died several days after the reviews of his Pathetic Symphony were released.

Turkeys can be separated by sex if you listen closely. Males grunt, females hiss.

The Tower of Pisa was built with a faulty foundation only ten feet deep. The building leans 17 feet right of center and continues to lean an additional ¼ inch each year.

Albert Fish, a mild-mannered house painter in New York City was arrested in 1934 and put to death. He had eaten 15 small children. His last victim was cooked in a stew.

Frank Bentenia of Middletown, Connecticut had three legs. He made his living with Ringling Brothers.

Frank Lentini, the King of the Freaks, had three legs, two sets of genitals, four feet, and sixteen toes. He could use his third leg as a sitting stool. Frank sired four normal children.

Beavers chew on wood for a reason. Chewing keeps their incisor teeth from growing too long and piercing their lower jaw; if this happens, the beaver cannot open his mouth to eat and promptly dies of starvation.

Myrtle Corbin from Texas had four legs. Half of another body grew between Myrtle's real legs. All four limbs were operational. Myrtle had five children despite her handicap.

Former slave Charley Smith was coaxed onto a slave ship in Africa because he was promised that in America "pancakes grow on trees."

Some construction workers were painting a sign in Wisconsin, labeling a large grain elevator. The weather got extremely cold and the men called it quits for the day. They did not get a chance to go back to their work on the large sign until the following spring because the Wisconsin winter took hold. This is the origin of the town named *Eleva*, Wisconsin.

The Gabon viper of Africa has the longest fangs of any poisonous snake. A specimen in the Philadelphia Zoo should have kept that in mind when it bit itself in the back in 1963. The poor creature died, of course, from its own deadly venom. Probably scratching an itch.

Robert Earl Hughes was a big man. He weighed 1,069 lbs. That was problem enough, but when he died he had to be buried in a piano case—there were no coffins large enough to fit him.

John Whitson, famous British adventurer, died as he galloped past a blacksmith's shop in England in 1629. Whitson fell from his steed and landed on a nail facing upwards on a board near the blacksmith shop.

A pig in Luneburg, Germany, had better luck. As a butcher knelt beside the porker to kill it with a pistol, the animal lashed out with its hooves and caused the executioner to shoot himself.

During the last primaries Nancy Reagan telephoned Ronnie while a television audience listened to her tell her husband that she was glad to be looking at all "the beautiful white people."

Seperation of Church and State.
"Why has Jesus Christ so far not succeeded in inducing the world to follow his teachings? . . . I am proposing a practical scheme to carry out his aims."—Woodrow Wilson.

The comments of France's Prime Minister Raymond Barre do not dissuade critics who claim France is a hotbed of anti-Semitism. He described the October, 1980 bombing of a synagogue in Paris as "this odious attack that was aimed at Jews and that struck at innocent Frenchmen."

"Segregation is not humiliating but a benefit, and ought to be so regarded by you gentlemen."—Woodrow Wilson to black leaders in 1913.

In the 1970s the Consumer Product Safety Commission ordered 80,000 buttons promoting "Toy Safety." The buttons turned out more dangerous than any toy could possibly be. They were sharp and coated with lethal lead paint.

19

English Quips

In Stroud, England, in 1981 a young girl died from a drug overdose. Her name was Jacqueline Rosser. As the mortician wheeled her corpse around, he noticed it was moving. Rosser was alive. She had been mistakenly declared dead in the hospital and moved to the mortuary.

Anna Mingo, an English chambermaid, escaped serious injury when she fell into a drainage shaft. "No doubt about it, my bust saved me," Anna said. Her measurements: 42-24-38.

Dismissing the city's contention that Gordon McLeod sat down too hard because he was drunk, a Glasgow court awarded Mr. McLeod damages for injuries sustained when a public toilet collapsed under his weight.

English historian Thomas May was so fat that he tied strings around his double chins to keep them from flapping. One day he swallowed a large mouthful and choked to death.

British playwright Thomas Otway was very poor and went several days without eating. He received one coin, spent it on food, and died choking on his first bite.

Businessman Peter Balfour recently wished newly-engaged Prince Charles "a long life and conjugal happiness with Lady Jane." Unfortunately for Mr. Balfour, the prince was not marrying Lady Jane Wellesley, but Lady Diana Spencer. Lady Jane had been a much publicized girlfriend of the prince.

In 1907 the British Navy constructed a ship called *The HMS Invincible*. The name could not have been less apt. One shot from a German cruiser in 1916 sank *The Invincible*.

Captain Bligh of the *Bounty* was not loved by his followers on land or sea. He is the only leader to have endured a mutiny on land as well as at sea. Sailors took command of his ship and soldiers took command of his office while he was governor of New South Wales.

American marketing genius Timothy Dexter once sent a ship full of coal to Newcastle, England, one of the leading English ports that ships coal around the world. Just at that time England was plagued by a coal strike and the ship full of coal heated all the homes in Newcastle. Dexter made a fast buck.

British literary critic Lionel Johnson fell off a barstool and died in 1902.

The Arab sheikhdom of Dubai bought a British snowplow from Bunce Ltd—for clearing sand.

A nun poured some tea for a famous Irish bishop and asked,
"How many lords, my lump?"

It seems English companies are very bold in their marketing strategies. Eastern Sands and Refractories of Cambridge once sent 1,800 tons of sand to Abu Dhabi—for filtration.

The label on the exhibit didn't fool a nine-year-old visitor to an English museum. They might call it a "Roman sesterce coin from between 135 and 138 A.D.," but he recognized it as a soft drink company's plastic token. Turned out the squirt was right.

John Keats, British Romantic poet, had syphilis.

Scottish folklorists tell this one (of course, it's true, every word): Warned by a soothsayer that he would die if he set foot on Irish soil, Lord Barclay of Kildonnen Castle shunned the Emerald Isle. So what was he to do when told that a mound of dirt he tripped over outside his castle entrance was ballast left by Irish fishermen? Why, what any self-respecting Scottish nobleman would do in the circumstances: he dropped dead then and there.

For the princely sum of 63,000 pounds (175,000 American dollars) English farmer James Dick bought a prize bull in 1963. When he put the magnificent beast to stud, however, Dick's bull didn't work: the animal was sterile.

Homing pigeon fanciers in Yorkshire, England entered a total of 20,000 birds in the annual race of the North Shore Federation. Somewhere along the 150-mile course 19,500 of the prize contestants disappeared, never to be seen again.

Waking up one morning to find a dead man stuck halfway through her bedroom window, a London spinster was intrigued by the mystery. Was he an admirer who had hoped to woo her? Probably not, the police concluded; more likely a burglar with a weak heart.

English police, searching for drugs, took along their trained drughounds "Laddie" and "Boy" while questioning some suspects. During the interrogation the suspects gently stroked the two dogs, who responded by going to sleep. When the cops got up to make the arrest, "Laddie" snarled menacingly at them and "Boy" bit one of his masters on the leg. The dogs are now retired.

The English governor of the New York and New Jersey colonies from 1702 to 1708 was a flamboyant homosexual. Edward Hyde, Viscount Cornbury, often wore female garb in public and he posed for his official portrait in a revealing evening gown. He was relieved of his duties in 1708—for taking bribes.

They talk about the luck of the Irish—two British brothers, identical twins in fact, died on the same road one hour apart from each other.

Credited as the first Englishman to wear suspenders, Lieutenant Andrew Bright never quite got the hang of them, it seems. Forgetting he had them on one day, Bright tried to take his trousers off while still wearing his jacket. Tangled in the galluses, he knocked over a candle and perished in the ensuing fire.

Mary Ann Smith of London was a forerunner of all the modern women who devise ingenious part-time jobs. Mary Ann was a human alarm clock for her poor neighbors who couldn't afford mechanical ones. She woke them up by shooting peas against their windows, for which they paid her a few pence a month.

When Ashford accused Thornton of killing his [Ashford's] sister in 1817, Thornton's response was that of an English gentleman. He challenged Ashford to a duel—not, however, with rapiers or sabers in the modern manner. What Thornton had in mind was medieval combat in full armor—with lances and broadswords— and he showed up at his chosen time and place prepared to do battle. Unnerved, Ashford absented himself from the contest, and Thornton claimed he was legally vindicated. Due to an oversight by Parliament, Ashford could no longer press his case. It seems trial by combat was still the law of the land.

Edward Stainer of Blaydon, England finally decided to locate the origin of a draft he had been feeling in his living room for years. He traced it to a spot under the floor, pried up the boards, and found himself looking down an ancient mineshaft 1000 feet deep.

Sir William Symonds, Surveyor of His Majesty's Navy, had this to say about propeller-driven ships in 1837: ". . . it would be found altogether useless in practice, because the power being applied in the stern, it would be absolutely impossible to make the vessel steer."

20

Miscellany

Endurance
After a series of major storms on the English seacost, Margate Pier was declared in danger of collapse, so a demolition crew was dispatched to finish it off. Several violent explosions later, the structure was still intact. When a second crew replaced the first demolition team, their efforts became a tourist attraction. After fifteen huge charges had been detonated, the pier was tilting slightly to starboard. They don't build 'em like they used to!

Completed in 1625 after 90 years of construction, the cathedral of Corcuetos, Spain, collapsed the day it was finished.

When the John Hancock Building was completed in Boston for $75 million, the architects' problems really began: a design defect caused windows on the upper floors to pop out and rain down on the streets far below, endangering cars and pedestrians. By the time the problem was solved four years later the cost had increased to $200 million, including $50 million in lost rents.

Joe Phillips of Sheffield, England, had finally done it—completed building the 62-foot steel boat he'd been working on for five years. He invited the whole town to attend the launching ceremony preceding the round-the-world cruise. On the appointed day a crowd of well-wishers showed up, including town officials and a band. The 26-ton yacht was christened with a bottle of rum and slipped down the ways. You guessed it: it kept slipping, right to the bottom.

If you closely examine a map of South Dakota, you'll see that the man-made western border of the state has a slight bump in it as it runs north-south. When the territory was being surveyed, the boundary was set to fall on the 27th meridian west from Washington, D.C. As the surveyors working down from the north met those coming up from the south, they missed each other by a few miles. This error remains on every map to this day.

Charles McCrary built a suspension bridge across the Snake River in Wyoming, constructed of old junk. As plans for the bridge he used a postcard of the San Francisco Bay Bridge.

In the Austria Fountain in Vienna there are five statues filled with cigars. Ludwig von Schwanthaler, the sculptor, tried to smuggle cigars in the bronze sculptures, but they were installed before he could remove the cigars.

In 1939 there was a proposal to build a 250-foot monument in Mount Battie, Maine, celebrating Captain Hansen Gregory. Captain Gregory invented the doughnut hole. The monument was never built.

Horse drawn carriages moved through New York City streets at an average speed of 11½ miles per hour in 1906. In 1972, automobile traffic moved at 8 miles per hour in the city.

Famous detective Allan Pinkerton died unexpectedly in 1884. While taking a brisk walk he fell, bit his tongue, and died of an infection in his mouth.

Famous Spanish composer Enrique Granados Campina was deathly afraid of sea travel. He was persuaded to come to America to hear an opera based on his music. He returned to Europe on the *S. S. Sussex* which was torpedoed by a German submarine in 1916.

In 1964 Gary Grannai escorted Tricia Nixon to the International Debutante Ball in New York City. Seven years later President Nixon was justifying his prosecution of the Vietnam War, despite the family's loss of a friend: "Gary was a second lieutenant. He was on patrol duty when it happened. You feel the personal tragedy when it comes into your own home. Yet there is no alternative to the war's going on." Publication of these remarks was followed by the reappearance of Gary Grannai, who was very much alive and happily married.

When Adam Smith, the great theoretician of free trade, was appointed a customs commissioner, he was put in an equivocal position: he had publicly espoused smuggling to avoid government interference in private business.

French industrialist Pierre Michelin died in a crash of his Citroen automobile in 1937. Police blamed his death on a defect in the car. Besides being an officer of the tire company bearing his name, Michelin had been a director of the Citroen Auto Co.

Off with his . . .
The English word *testimony* derives from the Roman practice of placing the right hand over the testicles when taking an oath. Don't ask what happened to men found guilty of perjury.

Leaning out his car window to yell "Sucker!" at a wedding party, a Canadian motorist plowed into a parked auto and was arrested.

223

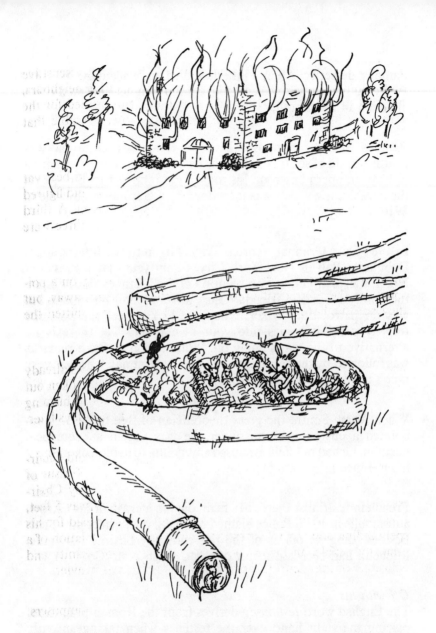

The fire volunteers arrived quickly when a blaze began at Converse College in Spartanburg, South Carolina in January, 1892. But by the time they cleared their seldom-used hoses of mouse nests, the institution had burned to the ground.

224

Tokyo resident Matsuzo Ohama proved to have fatally sensitive ears. Maddened by the persistent piano playing of his neighbors, he killed the mother and her two daughters. Imprisoned for the crime, the noise of his fellow convicts was so unbearable that Ohama requested and was granted an early execution.

A man in South Africa climbed into a huge abandoned beer vat to see what he could see. When he didn't reappear a friend figured he was enjoying himself and climbed in to join the fun. A third curious friend followed the pair. Some time later all three were found dead from poisonous fumes.

In 1980 an Australian toddler was discovered chewing on a poisonous snake. Her horrified parents snatched the snake away, but they needn't have worried: the little girl had already bitten the snake to death.

Little known is the fact that the ill-fated liner *Titanic* was already in trouble as it left its Southampton berth. A fire had broken out in one of the huge vessel's coal bunkers, and it was still burning when the ship hit an even larger iceberg and sank four days later.

For some reason the Chinese Communist party was afraid Chairman Mao would be compared to Adolf Hitler. In a 1960 issue of *National Construction*—a party magazine—an article by Chairman Mao was introduced in this way: "Adolf Hitler was 5 feet, 6 inches tall and weighed 143 pounds. He **was** renowned for his spellbinding oratory, relations with women, and annihilation of a minority people. In his last years he suffered from insanity and delusions of grandeur. Chairman Mao is taller and heavier.

Mieczyslaw Karlowicz was one of the greatest Polish composers. He was skiing in 1909 and was buried by an avalanche.

During a Gemini space flight Chet Huntley told a national viewing audience that "the Glenn *fight* was witnessed by the largest audience in history."

M. Cambon, the French Ambassador, thanked a Chicago mayor for a tour of Chicago. "Thank you," he said. "But I am sorry so to cockroach on your time." The Chicago mayor replied, "But you don't mean 'cockroach,' Mr. Cambon; it is 'encroach' you mean." "Oh, is it?" Cambon asked. "I see, a difference in gender."

Unprepared for the intense cold in the New World, more than half of the *Mayflower* passengers died in Plymouth, Massachusetts.

Mexican general Rudolfo Fierro died in 1917 when he decided to take a short-cut to Sonora and his horse sank in quicksand.

Wallingford Riegger was an American composer who died in 1961. Riegger was walking down the street and got tangled in the leashes of two dogs. He fell, cracked his skull and died.

Heywood Broun was a sloppy dresser. Once, as a war correspondent, he met General Pershing who asked, "Have you fallen down, Mr. Broun?"

To pay for the restoration of his fabulous estate of Monticello in Virginia, founding father Thomas Jefferson mortgaged all his slaves in 1796.